easy to make!
Healthy Meals in Minutes

Good Housekeeping

easy to make!
Healthy Meals in Minutes

COLLINS & BROWN

This edition published in Great Britain in 2011
by Collins & Brown
10 Southcombe Street
London W14 0RA

An imprint of Anova Books Company Ltd

The Good Housekeeping website is
www.goodhousekeeping.co.uk

10 9 8 7 6 5 4 3 2 1

ISBN 978-1-84340-649-5

A catalogue record for this book is available from the
British Library.

Reproduction by Dot Gradations Ltd
Printed by Times Printing, Malaysia.

This book can be ordered direct from the publisher.

www.anovabooks.com

NOTES

- Both metric and imperial measures are given for the recipes. Follow either set of measures, not a mixture of both, as they are not interchangeable.
- All spoon measures are level.
  1 tsp = 5ml spoon; 1 tbsp = 15ml spoon.
- Ovens and grills must be preheated to the specified temperature.
- Use sea salt and freshly ground black pepper unless otherwise suggested.
- Fresh herbs should be used unless dried herbs are specified in a recipe.
- Medium eggs should be used except where otherwise specified. Free-range eggs are recommended.
- Note that certain recipes, including mayonnaise, lemon curd and some cold desserts, contain raw or lightly cooked eggs. The young, elderly, pregnant women and anyone with an immune-deficiency disease should avoid these, because of the slight risk of salmonella.
- Calorie, fat and carbohydrate counts per serving are provided for the recipes.

Picture Credits
Photographer: Nicki Dowey
Home Economist: Lucy McKelvie
Stylist: Helen Trent
Additional Photography: Craig Robertson (Basics)

Contents

Foreword

Cooking, for me, is one of life's great pleasures. Not only is it necessary to fuel your body, but it exercises creativity, skill, social bonding and patience. The science behind the cooking also fascinates me, learning to understand how yeast works, or to grasp why certain flavours marry quite so well (in my mind) is to become a good cook.

I've often encountered people who claim not to be able to cook – they're just not interested or say they simply don't have time. My sister won't mind me saying that she was one of those who sat firmly in the camp of disinterested domestic goddess. But things change, she realised that my mother (an excellent cook) can't always be on hand to prepare steaming home-cooked meals and that she actually wanted to become a mother one day who was able to whip up good food for her own family. All it took was some good cook books (naturally, Good Housekeeping was present and accounted for) and some enthusiasm and sure enough she is now a kitchen wizard, creating such confections that even baffle me.

I've been lucky enough to have had a love for all things culinary since as long as I can remember. Baking rock-like chocolate cakes and misshapen biscuits was a right of passage that I protectively guard. I made my mistakes young, so have lost the fear of cookery mishaps. I think it's these mishaps that scare people, but when you realise that a mistake made once will seldom be repeated, then kitchen domination can start.

This Good Housekeeping Easy to Make! collection is filled with hundreds of tantalising recipes that have been triple tested (at least!) in our dedicated test kitchens. They have been developed to be easily achievable, delicious and guaranteed to work – taking the chance out of cooking.

I hope you enjoy this collection and that it inspires you to get cooking.

Meike.

Meike Beck
Cookery Editor
Good Housekeeping

0

The Basics

Eat well, stay well

'We are what we eat' – nutritionists from around the world agree that the food we eat has an important effect on our health and vitality. From the moment of conception and throughout life, diet plays a crucial role in helping us stay fit and healthy. A healthy balanced diet can protect against serious illnesses such heart disease and cancer, increase resistance to colds and other infections, boost energy levels, help combat the stresses of modern living and improve physical and mental performance.

Choose wisely

Our body needs over forty different nutrients to function and stay healthy. Some, such as carbohydrates, proteins and fats, are required in relatively large amounts; others, such as vitamins, minerals and trace elements, are required in minute amounts, but are nonetheless essential for health. No single food or food group provides all the nutrients we need, which is why we need to eat a variety of different foods. Making sure your body gets all the nutrients it needs is easy if you focus on foods that are nutrient rich and dump those highly refined and processed foods that provide lots of saturated fat, sugar and calories but not much else.

Ten principles of healthy eating

1 **Enjoy** your food
2 **Eat a variety** of different foods
3 **Eat the right amoun**t to be a healthy weight
4 **Eat plenty of foods** rich in carbohydrates and fibre; whenever possible, choose wholegrain cereals
5 **Eat at least 5 servings of fruit** and/or vegetables each day
6 **Keep sugary foods** and drinks as a treat rather than something you consume every day
7 **If you drink alcohol,** drink sensibly and stay within the safe guidelines, which are no more than 3 units of alcohol a day for women and no more than 4 units of alcohol a day for men, with at least one alcohol-free day a week
8 **Choose reduced- and low-fat** dairy products when possible
9 **Aim to drink** between 6 and 8 glasses of water a day
10 **Avoid adding salt** to food

Fruit and vegetables: five a day

One of the easiest ways to stay healthy is to eat plenty of fruit and vegetables. We can probably all remember being told by our parents to eat our 'greens' because they were good for us, and all the major reports on healthy eating have endorsed this good advice. It's no coincidence that in Mediterranean countries, where people eat almost twice the amount of fruit and vegetables that we do in the UK, they live longer and healthier lives. Fruit and vegetables contain an arsenal of disease-fighting compounds – vitamins, minerals, fibre and phytochemicals, which is why nutrition experts believe that they are the cornerstone of a healthy diet. The World Cancer Research Fund estimates that a diet rich in fruit and vegetables could prevent 20% of all cancer deaths, while The World Health Organisation estimates that 2.7 million deaths worldwide can be attributed to low fruit and vegetable intake. Eating a diet rich in fruit and vegetables can reduce the risk of a range of medical problems including heart disease, stroke, high blood pressure, certain types of cancer, cataracts and an eye condition called age-related macular degeneration, dementia and Alzheimer's disease.

Variety is key

Wherever we shop, most of us are lucky enough to have a wide range of different fruit and vegetables available to us, but do we really take advantage of the range? It's very easy to get stuck in a rut of buying the same things from one week to the next. Variety may be the spice of life, but it's also the key to a healthy diet and is particularly important when it comes to fruit and vegetables. Different coloured fruit and vegetables contain different vitamins, minerals and phytochemicals that help to keep you healthy in different ways, and so to make sure you get a good selection of all these nutrients you need to eat a variety of different produce. When you're buying fruit and vegetables don't just stick to your same old favourites – be adventurous and try something new. You'll find plenty of recipes to tempt you in this book.

Add colour to your meals

You probably already know that you should be eating at least five servings of fruit and vegetables a day, but did you know you should also be eating a rainbow? When you're planning meals, aim to fill your plate with colour – think of red, orange, yellow, green and purple fruit and vegetables and try to eat at least one serving from each of the colour bands every day.

Choosing the right carbohydrates

With the recent craze for low-carbohydrate diets, you may be forgiven for thinking that carbohydrates are best avoided. In fact, this couldn't be further from the truth. Most nutritionists agree that foods in this group are an important part of a healthy balanced diet. However, not all carbs are equal. Most of the vitamins and protective components in grains are concentrated in the bran and germ layers of the grain, but when grains are refined, as for instance in the production of white flour, the bran and germ are removed and most of the fibre and some of the nutrients are stripped away. This is why it is better to choose wholegrain carbohydrates such as brown rice and wholemeal bread over refined carbohydrates. Studies have shown that diets rich in wholegrain foods can reduce the risk of heart disease, stroke, certain types of cancer and Type 2 diabetes.

The Glycaemic Index

During the digestive process, carbohydrates need to be broken down into glucose – the simplest form of sugar – before they can be absorbed by your body. Recent research suggests the rate at which carbohydrates are broken down can also determine their healthiness. The Glycaemic Index (GI) is a system used for ranking carbohydrates according to how quickly they are broken down. Foods with a low GI (less than 55), such as lentils, apples and pears, are absorbed more slowly and steadily and generate a slow release of sugar into the bloodstream. Foods with a high GI (more than 70), such as cornflakes, bagels and soft drinks, are broken down into sugar quickly, which results in a sudden rush of sugar into the bloodstream. While this can be useful for athletes who need to replenish blood sugar after strenuous exercise, it is not necessary for the rest of us.

Diverse benefits

Although the GI diet was originally developed to help people with diabetes achieve better control of their blood sugar, the benefits are certainly not restricted to diabetics. Studies have shown that following a low-GI diet can help increase levels of 'good' cholesterol and reduce 'bad' cholesterol in the blood, which will help to reduce the risk of heart disease. Recent studies also show that people who ate a low glycaemic index diet lost more weight than people who ate a higher glycaemic index diet. The GI is only one measurement of what makes a food healthy. Other factors, such as the vitamin content and the amount of fat a food contains, will affect its overall healthiness. Foods that have a low to medium GI and are also low in sugar and fat are the best choice.

Fats – the healthy and no so healthy

Of all the nutrients in our diet fat must be the most debated and the most misunderstood. Although, in terms of healthy eating, fat is often cast as the villain, it's worth remembering that it also plays a beneficial role. In the body, fat cushions and protects the vital organs, provides energy stores and helps insulate the body. In the diet, it is necessary for the absorption of fat-soluble vitamins (A, D, E and K) and to provide essential fatty acids that the body can't make itself. While some fat is essential, many of us are eating too much of the wrong types of fat and not enough of the right types. A high-fat diet, particularly one that contains a lot of saturated 'animal' fats, is known to increase the risk of problems such as heart disease, stroke and certain types of cancer.

Polyunsaturated fats

Omega-6 fats These are mostly found in vegetable oils and margarines such as sunflower oil, safflower oil, corn oil and soya bean oil. Omega-6 fats help lower the LDL 'bad' cholesterol in the blood, but if you eat too much they will also lower the 'good' HDL cholesterol.
Omega-3 fats These are found mainly in oil-rich fish such as salmon, fresh tuna, mackerel and sardines, in linseeds (flax) and rapeseed oil. They help to protect the heart by making the blood less sticky and likely to clot, by lowering blood pressure, and by encouraging the muscles lining the artery walls to relax, thus improving blood flow to the heart. It's important to have a balance of omega-3 and

omega-6 fats in the diet. At the moment most of us have too much omega-6 fats and not enough omega-3 fats and recent research suggests that low levels of omega-3s in the blood may contribute to depression, antisocial behaviour and schizophrenia.

Monounsaturated fats

Monounsaturated fats are found mainly in olive oil, walnut oil and rapeseed oil, nuts and avocados. They can help reduce the risk of heart disease by lowering LDL 'bad' cholesterol.

Saturated fat

Saturated 'animal' fats are found in full fat dairy products (cheese, yogurt, milk, cream), lard, fatty cuts of meat and meat products such as sausages and burgers, pastry, cakes, biscuits, and coconut and palm oil. A diet high in saturated fats can raise levels of LDL 'bad' cholesterol in the blood, which will cause narrowing of the arteries and increase the risk of heart attacks and stroke.

Trans fats

Trans fats occur naturally in small amounts in meat and dairy products, but they are also produced during the process of hydrogenation that is used to convert liquid vegetable oils into semi-solid fats in the manufacture of some types of margarine. Trans fats are most commonly found in biscuits, cakes, pastries, meat pies, sausages, crackers and takeaway foods. Although chemically trans fats are still unsaturated fat, studies show that in the body they behave like saturated fat, causing blood cholesterol levels to rise; in fact, some studies suggest that trans fats are worse than saturated fats.

Eating more fibre

Despite the fact that it passes through the digestive tract largely undigested, fibre plays an important role in helping us stay fit and healthy. It helps keep our digestive tract in good working order and can also help reduce high blood cholesterol and keep blood sugar levels stable. Fibre can be divided into two groups – insoluble and soluble; both groups help keep the body healthy in a different way.

Insoluble fibre

Insoluble fibre, which is found mainly in wholegrain cereals but also in fruit, vegetables and pulses, helps to prevent constipation and problems such as haemorrhoids (piles) and diverticular disease. It works by absorbing water, making the stools larger, softer and easier to pass. Sometimes referred to as 'nature's broom', insoluble fibre also speeds the passage of waste material through the body. The faster waste materials are excreted, the less time potentially harmful substances have to linger in the bowel.

Soluble fibre

Soluble fibre, found in oats and oat bran, beans and pulses and some fruit and vegetables, helps to lower high blood cholesterol levels, which in turn will help reduce the risk of heart disease. Soluble fibre also helps to slow the absorption of sugar into the bloodstream, which makes foods rich in soluble fibre a good choice for people with diabetes or anyone trying to balance blood sugar levels.

Guideline Daily Amount (GDA)

The Guideline Daily Amount of fibre is 24g for adults and 15g for children aged between 5 and 10 years; to reach this target, most of us need to increase our fibre intake by about 50%.

Cutting down on salt

Reducing the amount of salt in our diet is, say health experts, one of the most important steps we can take to reduce the risk of high blood pressure, a condition that affects one in three adults in the UK. Experts have calculated that reducing our salt intake to 6g a day would reduce the number of people suffering from stroke by 22% and from heart attacks by 16%, saving around 34,000 lives each year.

Hidden salt

You may think the easiest way to cut back on salt is not to sprinkle salt over your food when you're at the table, but unfortunately the answer isn't quite that simple – only around 15% of the salt we eat comes from salt added to our food during cooking and at the table. Three-quarters of all the salt we consume is hidden in processed foods – one small tin of chicken soup, for instance, can contain well over half the recommended daily intake of salt for an adult.

Re-educating our taste buds

Our taste for salt is something we learn to like the more we eat. But just in the same way that we can teach our taste buds to enjoy foods with less sugar, we can train them to enjoy foods with less salt (sodium chloride). If you gradually reduce the amount of salt you eat, the taste receptors on the tongue become more sensitive to salt. This process takes between two and three weeks. Use herbs and spices to enhance the natural flavours of foods and before long you'll be enjoying the real taste of food – not the flavour of salt.

Special diets: dairy-free, wheat-free and gluten-free

In recent years there has been a growing awareness that for some people food allergy or intolerance can cause a range of health problems, including eczema, asthma, skin rashes, migraine and irritable bowel syndrome. Any food can provoke an allergic reaction, although some are more likely than others. Wheat and dairy products are two of the most common causes of food intolerance.

Dairy-free diets

The following is a list of foods to avoid on a dairy-free diet:

- Milk
- Cheese
- Yogurt
- Butter
- Most margarines and low-fat spreads
- Milk chocolate
- Cream
- Ice cream
- Fromage frais
- Dairy desserts

Many processed foods contain lactose (milk sugar) or traces of cow's milk protein, and there is a host of other names for ingredients derived from milk.

Avoid products that list any of the following words in the ingredients:

- Milk protein, milk, milk powder, skimmed milk powder
- Non-fat milk solids
- Animal fat
- Whey
- Casein or caseinate
- Hydrolysed casein or whey
- Lactose
- Lacalbumin
- Lactoglobulin
- Ghee

Calcium concern

Milk and dairy products are a major source of calcium in our diet. If you can't get enough calcium from your diet you may need to take a supplement. Check with a pharmacist that the supplement you choose does not contain lactose. Good non-dairy sources of calcium include: canned fish such as pilchards and sardines, dark green leafy vegetables such as spinach and watercress, bread, apricots, canned, fresh and dried beans, including baked beans, and hard water.

Wheat- and gluten-free diets

Many people are discovering that their body reacts badly when they eat wheat. Symptoms include bloating, IBS (irritable bowel syndrome), headaches and tiredness. Sometimes simply reducing your wheat intake can help; but some people may have to avoid wheat altogether. Coeliac disease is a more serious condition than wheat intolerance. It is caused by an intolerance to gluten, a protein found in wheat, rye, barley and oats. A gluten-free diet means cutting out wheat, oats, barley, rye and all products made using them. Products labelled as being wheat free are not necessarily gluten free because they may contain other gluten-containing grains. Equally, products labelled gluten free are not necessarily wheat free because they may contain wheat starch (gluten is a protein and people with a gluten intolerance don't have a problem with the starchy part of the grain).

Foods to avoid on a gluten-free diet include:

- Wheat, oats, barley, rye
- Wheat flour (white, wholemeal, self-raising)
- All foods made with wheat flour (bread, pasta, cakes, biscuits, crackers, pastry, batter, semolina, couscous)
- All products made with barley meal or flour
- All products made with rye meal or flour (rye bread or rye crispbread)
- All products containing oatmeal or oat flour
- Breakfast cereals containing wheat, bran, oats, barley
- Any dish that includes breadcrumbs
- Sausages, except 100% meat sausages and those labelled gluten-free
- Sauces and gravies thickened with flour
- Many manufactured goods contain flour as a thickening agent or filler so it is essential to check the label on individual products.

Substitute:

- Rice, corn, polenta (cornmeal), buckwheat, quinoa
- Rice, potato, soya, corn (maize) or chickpea flour
- Arrowroot, cornflour, sago or tapioca
- Cornflakes, Rice Crispies
- Rice or buckwheat noodles, gluten-free pasta
- Gluten-free bread or bread mix, puffed rice cakes, rice crackers, taco shells

Nutrition labelling

Two new sets of guidelines that claim to help us select a healthy balanced diet are currently in use. The traffic light scheme developed by the Food Standards Agency provides information on fat, saturated fat, sugar and salt and uses a red, amber or green colour coding to indicate whether a food is high, medium or low in these nutrients. The other scheme is based on Guideline Daily Amounts (GDAs) and gives an indication of how many calories, fat, salt, sugar and fibre a food contains and what it contributes to the amount of that nutrient you should eat in a day.

GDAs for adults

	Women	Men
Energy (calories)	2000	2500
Fat (g)	70	95
Saturated fat (g)	20	30
Total sugars (g)	90	120
Dietary fibre (g)	24	24
Sodium (g)	2.4	2.4
Salt	6	6

Assessing nutrients

Another quick and easy way to assess if a food is high or low in a particular nutrient is to use the table below. Look at the amount of a particular nutrient per serving or per 100g (3$\frac{1}{2}$oz) for snacks or cooking ingredients and check the table below to find out if it's high or low.

	High	Low
Fat	more than 20g	less than 3g
Saturated fat	more than 5g	less than 1g
Sugar	more than 10g	less than 2g
Fibre	more than 3g	less than 0.5g
Sodium	more than 0.5g	less than 0.1g
Salt	more than 1.3g	less than 0.3g

Making soups

Soups are nutritious, full of flavour and easy to make. Incredibly versatile, they can be smooth or chunky, light for a first course or substantial for a main course, made with vegetables, pulses, meat, chicken or fish.

Puréeing soups

1 **Using a jug blender** Allow the soup to cool slightly, then fill the jug about half full, making sure that there is more liquid than solids. Cover the lid with a teatowel and hold it on tightly. Blend until smooth, then add more solids and blend again until all the soup is smooth. (If you have a lot of soup, transfer each batch to a clean pan.)

2 **Using a stick blender** Allow the soup to cool slightly. Stick the blender deep into the soup, switch it on, and keep it moving so that all the soup is puréed.

3 **Using a mouli** The mouli-légumes makes a fine purée although it takes longer than using a blender. Fit the fine plate to the mouli-légumes and set it over a bowl with a teatowel underneath to keep it from moving on the table. Fill the bowl of the mouli about halfway, putting in more solids than liquid. Work in batches if you have a particularly large quantity of soup.

4 **Using a sieve** If you don't have a blender or mouli-légumes, you can purée soup by pushing it through a sieve, although this will take a much longer time.

Partially puréed soups

1 For an interesting texture, purée one-third to half of the ingredients, then stir back into the soup.

2 Alternatively, prepare the vegetables or other ingredients, but set aside a few choice pieces. While the soup is cooking, steam or boil these pieces until just tender; refresh green vegetables in cold water. Just before serving, cut into smaller pieces and add to the soup.

Chunky soups

1 Cut the ingredients into bite-sized pieces. Heat oil or butter in the soup pan and cook the onions – and garlic if you like – until soft and lightly coloured.

2 Add the remaining ingredients, putting in those that need the longest cooking first. Pour in some stock and bring to the boil.

3 Simmer gently until all the ingredients are tender. If too much liquid cooks away, just add more.

Simple vegetable soup

You can use almost any mixture of vegetables.
To serve four, you will need:
1 or 2 finely chopped onions, 2 tbsp oil or 1 tbsp oil and 25g (1oz) butter, 1 or 2 crushed garlic cloves (optional), 450g (1lb) chopped mixed vegetables, such as leeks, potatoes, celery, fennel, canned tomatoes and parsnip (chopped finely or cut into larger dice for a chunky soup), 1.1 litres (2 pints) stock.

1 Fry the onions in the oil or oil and butter until soft, and add the garlic cloves if you like.

2 Add the chopped mixed vegetables and the stock. Bring to the boil and simmer for 20–30 minutes until the vegetables are tender.

3 Leave chunky, partially purée or blend until smooth.

Basmati rice

1 Put the rice in a bowl and cover with cold water. Stir until this becomes cloudy, then drain and repeat until the water is clear.

2 Drain the rice before cooking.

Cooking rice and grains

There are two main types of rice: long-grain and short-grain. Long-grain rice is generally served as an accompaniment, while short-grain rice is used for dishes such as risotto, sushi and paella. Long-grain rice needs no special preparation, although basmati should be washed to remove excess starch.

Cooking rice

1 Use 50–75g (2–3oz) raw rice per person; measured by volume 50–75ml (2–2½ fl oz). Measure the rice by volume and put it in a pan with a pinch of salt and twice the volume of boiling water (or stock).

2 Bring to the boil. Turn the heat down to low, and set the timer for the time stated on the pack. The rice should be al dente: tender with a bite at the centre.

3 When the rice is cooked, fluff up the grains with a fork.

Cooking other grains

With any grain, the cooking time depends on how the grain has been processed. Both bulgur wheat and barley come in several forms, so you need to check which type you have bought.

Bulgur wheat

A form of cracked wheat, bulgur has had some or all of the bran removed. It is pre-boiled during manufacturing and may be boiled, steamed or soaked. It is good served as an accompaniment or used in salads.

1 **Simmering bulgur** Put in a pan with water to cover by about 2.5cm (1in). Bring to the boil, then simmer for 10–15 minutes until just tender. Drain well.

2 **Steaming bulgur** Place the bulgur in a steamer lined with a clean teatowel and steam over boiling water for 20 minutes or until the grains are soft.

3 **Soaking bulgur** Put the bulgur in a deep bowl. Cover with hot water and mix with a fork. Leave to steep for 20 minutes, checking to make sure there is enough water. Drain and fluff up with a fork.

Barley

There are three types of barley, all of which may be cooked on their own, or in a soup or stew.

1 **Whole barley** Soak the barley overnight in twice the volume of water, then drain well. Put the barley in a heavy-based pan, pour over boiling water and simmer for about 1½ hours or until tender. Check the liquid, adding more if necessary.

2 **Scotch (pot) barley** Rinse well, then simmer gently in boiling water for 45–50 minutes until tender.

3 **Pearl barley** This has had all of its outer husk removed, and needs no soaking. Rinse the barley and put it in a pan with twice the volume of water. Bring to the boil. Turn down the heat and simmer until tender, 25–30 minutes.

Couscous

Often mistaken for a grain, couscous is actually a type of pasta that originated in North Africa. It is perfect for serving with stews and casseroles, or making into salads. The tiny pellets do not require cooking and can simply be soaked.

1 Measure the couscous in a jug and add 1½ times the volume of hot water or stock. Cover the bowl and leave to soak for 5 minutes. Fluff up with a fork before serving.

2 If using for a salad, leave the couscous to cool completely before adding the other salad ingredients.

Quinoa

This nutritious South American grain makes a great alternative to rice.

1 Put the quinoa in a bowl of cold water. Mix well, soak for 2 minutes, then drain. Put in a pan with twice its volume of water. Bring to the boil.

2 Simmer for 20 minutes. Remove from the heat, cover and leave to stand for 10 minutes.

Wheat grain

Also known as whole wheat and wheat berries, wheat grain needs to be soaked overnight before simmering. You can sometimes find pre-cooked varieties that will cut down on soaking and cooking time.

1 Soak the wheat grain overnight in twice the volume of water, then drain well.

2 Measure the grain in a measuring cup, then put in a heavy-based pan with twice the volume of water (or use unsalted stock instead of water to add flavour).

3 Bring to the boil and simmer until tender, about 45 minutes. Check the liquid regularly to make sure it is not boiling away, and add more if necessary. Drain well.

Cooking beans

1 Pick through the beans to remove any grit or small stones.

2 Put the beans in a bowl or pan and pour over cold water to cover generously. Leave to soak for at least 8 hours, then drain. (If you are in a hurry, pour over boiling water and leave the beans to cool in the water for 1–2 hours.)

3 Put the soaked beans in a large pan and add water to cover by at least 5cm (2in). Bring to the boil and boil rapidly for 10 minutes.

4 Skim off the scum that rises to the top, turn down the heat and leave to simmer until the beans are soft inside. They should be tender but not falling apart. Check the water periodically to make sure there's enough to keep the beans well covered. Drain well. If using in a salad, allow to cool completely.

Using beans and lentils

Many dried beans and peas need to be soaked overnight before cooking. However, lentils do not need soaking and are quicker to cook. Quicker still are canned beans: they are ready to use, but should be drained in a sieve and rinsed in cold water first.

Cooking times

Times vary for different dried beans, peas and lentils. Older beans will take longer to cook, so use them within their 'best before' date.

Chickpeas	1–2 hours
Red kidney, cannellini, borlotti, butter, flageolet beans	1–3 hours
Red lentils	20 minutes
Green lentils	30–40 minutes

Sprouting beans

Mung beans, green or Puy lentils and alfalfa are all popular for home sprouting and are good in salads and stir-fries. You will only need about 3 tbsp beans to sprout at one time.

1 Pick through the beans to remove any grit or stones, then soak in cold water for at least 8 hours. Drain and place in a clean (preferably sterilised) jar. Cover the top with a dampened piece of clean cloth, secure and leave in a warm, dark place.

2 Rinse the sprouting beans twice a day. The sprouts can be eaten when there is about 1cm (½ in) of growth, or they can be left to grow for a day or two longer. When they are sprouted, leave the jar on a sunny windowsill for about 3 hours – this will improve both their flavour and their nutrients. Then rinse and dry them well. They can be kept for about three days in the refrigerator. Always rinse the beans well before using them.

Storing beans

Always store dried beans, peas and lentils in airtight containers in a cool, dry place. Use within 1 year – or check the 'best before' date. Do not mix old and new beans because they will take different times to cook.

Zesting citrus fruits

1 Wash and thoroughly dry the fruit. Using a vegetable peeler or sharp knife, cut away the zest (the coloured outer layer of skin), taking care to leave behind the bitter white pith. Remove as much zest as you need.

2 Stack the slices of zest on a board and shred or dice as required.

Preparing fruit

Nutritionally, fruit is important – both as a source of dietary fibre and of minerals and vitamins, especially vitamin C. Some varieties, especially apricots, mangoes and peaches, also provide vitamin A in the form of carotene. All fruits provide some energy, in the form of fructose (or fruit sugar), but most varieties are very low in fat and therefore low in calories. A few simple techniques can make preparing both familiar and not-so-familiar fruits quick and easy.

Segmenting citrus fruits

1 Cut off a slice at both ends of the fruit, then cut off the peel, just inside the white pith.

2 Hold the fruit over a bowl to catch the juice and cut between the segments just inside the membrane to release the flesh. Continue until all the segments are removed. Squeeze the juice from the membrane into the bowl and use as required.

Preparing pineapple

1 Cut off the base and crown of the pineapple, and stand the fruit on a chopping board.

2 Using a medium-sized knife, peel away a section of skin, going just deep enough to remove all or most of the hard, inedible 'eyes' on the skin. Repeat all the way around.

3 Use a small knife to cut out any remaining traces of the eyes.

4 Cut the peeled pineapple into slices.

5 You can buy special tools for coring pineapples but a 7.5cm (3in) biscuit cutter or an apple corer works just as well. Place the biscuit cutter directly over the core and press down firmly. If using an apple corer, cut out the core in pieces, as it will be too wide to remove in one piece.

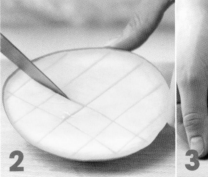

Preparing mangoes

1 Cut a slice to one side of the stone in the centre. Repeat on the other side.

2 Cut parallel lines into the flesh of one slice, almost to the skin. Cut another set of lines to cut the flesh into squares.

3 Press on the skin side to turn the fruit inside out, so that the flesh is thrust outwards. Cut off the chunks as close as possible to the skin. Repeat with the other half.

Preparing papaya

1 If using in a salad, peel the fruit using a swivel-headed vegetable peeler, then gently cut in half using a sharp knife. Remove the seeds using a teaspoon and slice the flesh, or cut into cubes.

2 If serving on its own, halve the fruit lengthways using a sharp knife, and use a teaspoon to scoop out the shiny black seeds and fibres inside the cavity.

Making smoothies and purées

Fruit, either cooked or raw, can be transformed into a smooth sauce by puréeing. Fruit also makes a healthy breakfast or snack that is bursting with flavour when used in a smoothie.

Puréeing in a blender

Some fruit can be puréed raw, while others are better cooked. Leave cooked fruit to cool before puréeing.

1 Put a large spoonful of fruit in the jug and blend until smooth, then add another spoonful and blend again. Add rest of fruit in batches.

2 For a very smooth purée, pass the fruit through a fine sieve.

Puréeing using a mouli

The fine plate of a mouli-légumes does a good job of puréeing, although it is slightly more laborious than a blender.

1 Set the mouli over a bowl and, working in batches, ladle in the fruit.

2 Turn the handle until the fruit has gone through, then repeat until all the fruit has been puréed.

Using fruit

Most fruit tastes marvellous raw, although a few always need to be cooked. Nearly all fruits make superb desserts when they are baked, poached or stewed, and many are equally good made into smoothies.

Good fruits for baking

Fruit	Preparation
Apples (dessert or cooking)	cored and halved or quartered
Apricots	whole or halved and stoned
Bananas	peeled and halved, or in their skins
Berries	whole
Nectarines and peaches	halved and stoned
Pears	cored and halved or quartered
Pineapple	cored and cut into large chunks
Plums	whole or halved and stoned

Basic smoothie

To serve four, you will need:
4 passion fruit, 150g (5oz) low-fat yogurt, 4 bananas, 225g (8oz) grapes.

1 Halve the passion fruit and scoop the pulp into a blender. Add the remaining ingredients. Crush 8 ice cubes and add to the blender.

2 Process until smooth and pour into glasses. Serve immediately.

Grilling

Cooking fruit under the grill is a quick and delicious method for fruit such as pineapple, peaches and figs.

1 Preheat the grill to high. Prepare the fruit and put in the grill pan (or a roasting tin) in a single layer. Sprinkle generously with sugar.

2 Set the grill pan under the grill about 10cm (4in) from the heat. Grill until the top is lightly caramelised and the fruit has softened, 5–8 minutes.

Baking

The key to success to baking fruit is in keeping the cooking time short, so that the delicate flesh of the fruit doesn't break down completely. Preheat the oven to 200°C (180°C fan oven) mark 6.

1 Prepare the fruit and put in a single layer in a buttered baking dish or individual dishes. Put a splash of water in the bottom of the dish(es). (For extra flavour, you can use fruit juice or wine instead of water.) Sprinkle the tops with sugar (and other flavourings such as spices, citrus zest or vanilla, if you like). Dot with butter.

2 Bake the fruit until just tender when pierced with a knife or skewer; this should take 15–25 minutes depending on the fruit and the size of the pieces. Leave to rest for a few minutes before serving.

Poached fruit

To serve four, you will need:
300g (11oz) sugar, 450g (1lb) fruit (pears, plums, peaches, nectarines, apricots), juice of 1 lemon.

1 Put the sugar in a large measuring jug and fill with cold water to make 1 litre (1½ pints). Transfer to a pan and heat gently, stirring now and then, until the sugar has dissolved.

2 Peel and halve the fruit, core pears, remove the stones from stone fruit, and gently toss with lemon juice.

3 Bring the sugar syrup to a simmer in a wide-based pan. Put in the fruit, cut sides down. It should be completely covered with syrup; add a little more water if necessary.

4 Simmer very gently for 30–40 minutes until soft when pierced with a knife. Serve hot or cold.

Stewed fruit

To serve four, you will need:
450g (1lb) prepared fruit (chunks of apples and rhubarb, whole gooseberries, halved plums), 1 tbsp lemon juice, sugar to taste.

1 Put the fruit in a non-stick stainless steel pan with the lemon juice and sugar. Add 2 tbsp water. Bring to the boil over a medium heat, then turn down the heat and simmer gently, partly covered, until the fruit is soft, stirring often.

Bread basics

Baking bread is one of the greatest pleasures of the kitchen, and one of the simplest. A basic loaf provides the foundation for almost infiniite variations, using different flours, creating different shapes, adding seeds, nuts, herbs and other flavourings.

Basic ingredients:

Yeast Fresh yeast is activated when blended with warm liquid. Dried yeast needs sugar to activate it (no sugar is needed if using milk): blend the yeast with a little of the water plus sugar (or milk) and leave for 15 minutes to froth. Fast-action (easy-blend) dried yeast is sprinkled directly into the flour and the liquid added afterwards. As a rough guide, for 700g (1½lb) flour use 15g (½oz) fresh yeast, 1 tbsp dried yeast or a 7g sachet (2 tsp) fast-action dried yeast.

Liquid This needs to be slightly warm to the fingertips. Milk gives bread a softer texture than water.

Flour Use strong white or wholemeal flour, or Granary flour.

Salt This controls fermentation, strengthens the gluten, which gives the bread its texture, and adds flavour.

Fats Some recipes include fat for flavour and to improve keeping quality.

To ensure good results:

Make sure shaped dough has risen sufficiently – usually to double its original size.

Always oil or flour the loaf tin or baking sheet, to prevent sticking.

Make sure the oven is at the correct temperature before baking.

Bake on a preheated ceramic baking stone (from good kitchen shops) if possible, even if the bread is in a loaf tin. The heat of the stone will give the bread a crisp base.

Cooling

If baked bread is left for too long either in the loaf tin or on the baking sheet, steam will gather and, as a result, the underneath will start to become soggy. To prevent this, always remove the loaf immediately and put it on a wire rack. Then leave it to cool completely before slicing.

Potential problems

The loaf hasn't risen enough:
- Not enough liquid was added.
- The yeast was not fresh.
- The dough was left to prove (rise) for too long, causing it to collapse during baking.

The loaf is too dense in texture:
- The dough was not kneaded long enough.
- The dough was not allowed to rise for long enough.
- Not enough, or too little, liquid was added.

Classic brown loaf

You will need:
300g (11oz) strong white bread flour, 200g (7oz) strong wholemeal flour, 15g (1/2oz) fresh yeast or 1 tsp dried yeast, 2 tsp salt.

1 Sift the flours into a bowl, make a well in the centre and pour in 325ml (11fl oz) warm water. Sprinkle over the yeast and mix in a little of the flour to make a batter. Sprinkle salt over the dry flour, so that it doesn't come into contact with the yeast. Cover and leave for 20 minutes.

2 Mix to a soft dough and knead for 10 minutes until smooth and elastic. Shape into a ball and place in a lightly oiled bowl. Cover and leave for 45 minutes–1½ hours until doubled in size.

3 Put the dough on a lightly floured surface and knock back by pressing with your knuckles to expel the air. Knead for 2–3 minutes, then shape and put into a greased 900g (2lb) loaf tin or on a lightly floured baking sheet. Cover and leave to rise for 45 minutes–1½ hours until doubled in size.

4 Preheat the oven to 200°C (180°C fan oven) mark 6. Bake for 50 minutes–1 hour if using a loaf tin, or 45–50 minutes on a baking sheet.

5 Tap the bottom of the loaf with your knuckles: if it is cooked it should sound hollow. Leave to cool on a wire rack.

Food storage and hygiene

Storing food properly and preparing it in a hygienic way is important to ensure that food remains as nutritious and flavourful as possible, and to reduce the risk of food poisoning.

Hygiene

When you are preparing food, always follow these important guidelines:

Wash your hands thoroughly before handling food and again between handling different types of food, such as raw and cooked meat and poultry. If you have any cuts or grazes on your hands, be sure to keep them covered with a waterproof plaster.

Wash down worksurfaces regularly with a mild detergent solution or multi-surface cleaner.

Use a dishwasher if available. Otherwise, wear rubber gloves for washing-up, so that the water temperature can be hotter than unprotected hands can bear. Change drying-up cloths and cleaning cloths regularly. Note that leaving dishes to drain is more hygienic than drying them with a teatowel.

Keep raw and cooked foods separate, especially meat, fish and poultry. Wash kitchen utensils in between preparing raw and cooked foods. Never put cooked or ready-to-eat foods directly on to a surface which has just had raw fish, meat or poultry on it.

Keep pets out of the kitchen if possible; or make sure they stay away from worksurfaces. Never allow animals on to worksurfaces.

Shopping

Always choose fresh ingredients in prime condition from stores and markets that have a regular turnover of stock to ensure you buy the freshest produce possible.

Make sure items are within their 'best before' or 'use by' date. (Foods with a longer shelf life have a 'best before' date; more perishable items have a 'use by' date.)

Pack frozen and chilled items in an insulated cool bag at the check-out and put them into the freezer or refrigerator as soon as you get home.

During warm weather in particular, buy perishable foods just before you return home. When packing items at the check-out, sort them according to where you will store them when you get home – the refrigerator, freezer, storecupboard, vegetable rack, fruit bowl, etc. This will make unpacking easier – and quicker.

The storecupboard

Although storecupboard ingredients will generally last a long time, correct storage is important:

Always check packaging for storage advice – even with familiar foods, because storage requirements may change if additives, sugar or salt have been reduced.

Check storecupboard foods for their 'best before' or 'use by' date and do not use them if the date has passed.

Keep all food cupboards scrupulously clean and make sure food containers and packets are properly sealed.

Once opened, treat canned foods as though fresh. Always transfer the contents to a clean container, cover and keep in the refrigerator. Similarly, jars, sauce bottles and cartons should be kept chilled after opening. (Check the label for safe storage times after opening.)

Transfer dry goods such as sugar, rice and pasta to moisture-proof containers. When supplies are used up, wash the container well and thoroughly dry before refilling with new supplies.

Store oils in a dark cupboard away from any heat source as heat and light can make them turn rancid and affect their colour. For the same reason, buy olive oil in dark green bottles.

Store vinegars in a cool place; they can turn bad in a warm environment.

Store dried herbs, spices and flavourings in a cool, dark cupboard or in dark jars. Buy in small quantities as their flavour will not last indefinitely.

Store flours and sugars in airtight containers.

Refrigerator storage

Fresh food needs to be kept in the cool temperature of the refrigerator to keep it in good condition and discourage the growth of harmful bacteria. Store day-to-day perishable items, such as opened jams and jellies, mayonnaise and bottled sauces, in the refrigerator along with eggs and dairy products, fruit juices, bacon, fresh and cooked meat (on separate shelves), and salads and vegetables (except potatoes, which don't suit being stored in the cold). A refrigerator should be kept at an operating temperature of 4–5°C.

It is worth investing in a refrigerator thermometer to ensure the correct temperature is maintained. To ensure your refrigerator is functioning effectively for safe food storage, follow these guidelines:

To avoid bacterial cross-contamination, store cooked and raw foods on separate shelves, putting cooked foods on the top shelf. Ensure that all items are well wrapped.

Never put hot food into the refrigerator, as this will cause the internal temperature of the refrigerator to rise.

Avoid overfilling the refrigerator, as this restricts the circulation of air and prevents the appliance from working properly.

It can take some time for the refrigerator to return to the correct operating temperature once the door has been opened, so don't leave it open any longer than is necessary.

Clean the refrigerator regularly, using a specially formulated germicidal refrigerator cleaner. Alternatively, use a weak solution of bicarbonate of soda: 1 tbsp to 1 litre (1³⁄₄ pints) water.

If your refrigerator doesn't have an automatic defrost facility, defrost regularly.

Maximum refrigerator storage times

For pre-packed foods, always adhere to the 'use by' date on the packet. For other foods the following storage times should apply, providing the food is in prime condition when it goes into the refrigerator and that your refrigerator is in good working order:

Vegetables and Fruit

Green vegetables	3–4 days
Salad leaves	2–3 days
Hard and stone fruit	3–7 days
Soft fruit	1–2 days

Dairy Food

Cheese, hard	1 week
Cheese, soft	2–3 days
Eggs	1 week
Milk	4–5 days

Fish

Fish	1 day
Shellfish	1 day

Raw Meat

Bacon	7 days
Game	2 days
Joints	3 days
Minced meat	1 day
Offal	1 day
Poultry	2 days
Raw sliced meat	2 days
Sausages	3 days

Cooked Meat

Joints	3 days
Casseroles/stews	2 days
Pies	2 days
Sliced meat	2 days
Ham	2 days
Ham, vacuum-packed (or according to the instructions on the packet)	1–2 weeks

1

Start the Day

Try Something Different

Instead of mango, use 2 nectarines or peaches, or 175g (6oz) soft seasonal fruits such as raspberries, strawberries or blueberries.

Mango and Oat Smoothie

150g (5oz) natural yogurt

1 small mango, peeled, stoned and chopped

2 tbsp oats

4 ice cubes

1 Put the yogurt into a blender. Set aside a little chopped mango to garnish if you like, and add the remaining mango, oats and ice cubes to the yogurt, and blend until smooth. Serve immediately, garnished with chopped mango.

Serves	EASY		NUTRITIONAL INFORMATION	
2	**Preparation Time** 5 minutes		**Per Serving** 145 calories, 2g fat (of which 1g saturates), 27g carbohydrate, 0.2g salt	Vegetarian

▼ Start the day: **Summer Berry Smoothie**

▶ Lunch: **Sprouted Bean and Mango Salad (see page 53)**

▶ Supper: **Chickpea Curry (see page 67)**

▶ Pudding: **Watermelon with Feta and Honey (see page 116)**

Summer Berry Smoothie

2 large, ripe bananas, about 450g (1lb), peeled and chopped

150g (5oz) natural yogurt

150ml (¼ pint) spring water

500g (1lb 2oz) fresh or frozen summer berries

1 Put the bananas, yogurt and spring water into a food processor or blender and whiz until smooth. Add the frozen berries and whiz to a purée.

2 Sieve the mixture into a large jug, using the back of a ladle to press it through. Pour into glasses and serve.

EASY	NUTRITIONAL INFORMATION		Serves
Preparation Time 10 minutes	**Per Serving** 107 calories, 1g fat (of which trace saturates), 24g carbohydrate, 0.1g salt	Vegetarian Gluten free	**6**

Apple and Almond Yogurt

500g (1lb 2oz) natural yogurt
50g (2oz) flaked almonds
50g (2oz) sultanas
2 apples

1 Put the yogurt in a bowl and add the almonds and sultanas.

2 Grate the apples, add to the bowl and mix together. Chill in the refrigerator overnight. Use as a topping for cereal.

Serves 4	EASY		NUTRITIONAL INFORMATION	
	Preparation Time 5 minutes, plus overnight chilling		**Per Serving** 193 calories, 8g fat (of which 1g saturates), 22g carbohydrate, 0.3g salt	Vegetarian Gluten free

Cook's Tip

Put the apples, lemon juice, sugar and water into a microwave-safe bowl, cover loosely with clingfilm and cook on full power in an 850W microwave for 4 minutes or until the apples are just soft.

250g (9oz) cooking apples, peeled and chopped

juice of ½ lemon

1 tbsp golden caster sugar

ground cinnamon

Apple Compote

To serve

25g (1oz) raisins

25g (1oz) chopped almonds

1 tbsp natural yogurt

1 Put the cooking apples into a pan with the lemon juice, caster sugar and 2 tbsp cold water. Cook gently for 5 minutes or until soft. Transfer to a bowl.

2 Sprinkle a little ground cinnamon over the top, cool and chill. It will keep for up to three days.

3 Serve with the raisins, chopped almonds and yogurt.

EASY		NUTRITIONAL INFORMATION		Serves
Preparation Time 10 minutes, plus chilling	**Cooking Time** 5 minutes	**Per Serving** 188 calories, 7g fat (of which 1g saturates), 29g carbohydrate, 0g salt	Vegetarian Gluten free	2

▼ Start the day: **Granola**
▶ Lunch: **Tuna, Bean and Red Onion Salad (see page 55)**
▶ Supper: **Pork and Noodle Stir-fry (see page 80)**
▶ Pudding: **Papaya with Lime Syrup (see page 113)**

Granola

300g (11oz) porridge oats

50g (2oz) chopped Brazil nuts

50g (2oz) flaked almonds

50g (2oz) wheatgerm or rye flakes

50g (2oz) sunflower seeds

25g (1oz) sesame seeds

100ml (3½fl oz) sunflower oil

3 tbsp clear honey

100g (3½oz) raisins

100g (3½oz) dried cranberries

1 Preheat the oven to 140°C (120°C fan oven) mark 1. Put the oats, nuts, wheatgerm or rye flakes, and all the seeds in a bowl. Gently heat the oil and honey in a pan. Pour it over the oats and stir to combine. Spread on a shallow baking tray and cook in the oven for 1 hour or until golden, stirring once. Cool briefly.

2 Transfer to a bowl and stir in the dried fruit. Store in an airtight container – the granola will keep for up to a week. Serve with milk or yogurt.

Makes	EASY		NUTRITIONAL INFORMATION	
15 servings	**Preparation Time** 5 minutes	**Cooking Time** 1 hour 5 minutes	**Per Serving** 254 calories, 14g fat (of which 2g saturates), 28g carbohydrate, 0g salt	Vegetarian Dairy free

Health Tip

Oats contain gluten and, strictly speaking, are not suitable for coeliacs. However, because they contain much smaller amounts than wheat, rye or barley, research shows that most people with coeliac disease can safely eat moderate amounts. The oats must be from sources where there is no risk of contamination from wheat or wheat products during processing or packing. As individual tolerances to gluten vary, if you are a coeliac, seek expert advice before eating oats.

Energy-boosting Muesli

500g (1lb 2oz) porridge oats
100g (3¹/₂oz) toasted almonds, chopped
2 tbsp pumpkin seeds
2 tbsp sunflower seeds
100g (3¹/₂oz) ready-to-eat dried apricots, chopped

1 Mix together the oats, almonds, seeds and apricots. Store in a sealable container for up to one month. Serve with milk or yogurt.

EASY	NUTRITIONAL INFORMATION		Makes
Preparation Time 5 minutes	**Per Serving** 208 calories, 9g fat (of which trace saturates), 28g carbohydrate, 0g salt	Vegetarian Dairy free	**15** **servings**

Porridge with Dried Fruit

200g (7oz) porridge oats

400ml (14fl oz) milk

75g (3oz) mixture of chopped dried figs, apricots and raisins

1 Put the oats into a large pan and add the milk and 400ml (14fl oz) water. Stir in the chopped dried figs, apricots and raisins, and heat gently, stirring until the porridge thickens and the oats are cooked.

2 Divide among four bowls and serve with a splash of milk.

Serves	EASY		NUTRITIONAL INFORMATION	
4	**Preparation Time** 5 minutes	**Cooking Time** 5 minutes	**Per Serving** 279 calories, 6g fat (of which 1g saturates), 49g carbohydrate, 0.2g salt	Vegetarian

Health Tip

Blueberries are an excellent fruit for healthy breakfasts. Research has shown that blueberries are one of the best sources of antioxidants. They may even help to protect against ageing and ageing diseases, and to reduce high cholesterol levels. They also help to keep the gut and urinary tract healthy.

Breakfast Bruschetta

1 ripe banana

250g (9oz) blueberries

200g (7oz) Quark

4 slices pumpernickel or wheat-free wholegrain bread

1 tbsp runny honey

1 Slice the banana and put into a bowl with the blueberries. Spoon in the Quark and mix well.

2 Toast the slices of bread on both sides, then spread with the blueberry mixture. Drizzle with the honey and serve immediately.

EASY		NUTRITIONAL INFORMATION		Serves
Preparation Time 5 minutes	**Cooking Time** 5 minutes	**Per Serving** 145 calories, 1g fat (of which 0g saturates), 30g carbohydrate, 0.4g salt	Vegetarian	**4**

Try Something Different

This will be just as good with toasted soda bread or seeded bread, mixed beans instead of borlotti or cannellini, and grated Gruyère or Cheddar instead of Parmesan.

Beans on Toast

1 tbsp olive oil

2 garlic cloves, finely sliced

400g can borlotti or cannellini beans

400g can chickpeas

400g can chopped tomatoes

leaves from 2 fresh rosemary sprigs

4 thick slices Granary bread

25g (1oz) Parmesan

chopped fresh parsley to serve

1 Heat the oil in a pan over a low heat, add the garlic and cook for 1 minute, stirring gently.

2 Drain and rinse the beans and chickpeas, add to the pan with the tomatoes, and bring to the boil. Chop the rosemary leaves finely and add to the pan. Reduce the heat and simmer for 8–10 minutes until thickened.

3 Meanwhile, toast the bread and put on to plates. Grate the Parmesan into the bean mixture, stir once, then spoon over the bread. Serve immediately, scattered with parsley.

Serves 4	EASY		NUTRITIONAL INFORMATION	
	Preparation Time 5 minutes	**Cooking Time** 10 minutes	**Per Serving** 364 calories, 9g fat (of which 2g saturates), 55g carbohydrate, 2.1g salt	Vegetarian

Try Something Different

Replace the hazelnuts with walnuts or pecan nuts and use sultanas instead of apricots.

75g (3oz) hazelnuts

450g (1lb) strong Granary bread flour

1 tsp salt

25g (1oz) butter, diced, plus extra to grease

75g (3oz) ready-to-eat dried apricots, chopped

2 tsp fast-action (easy-blend) dried yeast

2 tbsp molasses

about 225ml (8fl oz) hand-hot water

milk to glaze

Apricot and Hazelnut Bread

1 Spread the hazelnuts over a baking sheet. Toast under a hot grill until golden brown, turning frequently. Put the hazelnuts in a clean teatowel and rub off the skins. Cool, then chop them.

2 Put the flour into a large bowl. Add the salt, then rub in the butter. Stir in the hazelnuts, dried apricots and dried yeast.

3 Make a well in the middle and gradually work in the molasses and about 225ml (8fl oz) hand-hot water to form a soft dough, adding a little more water if the dough feels dry.

4 Knead for 8–10 minutes until smooth, then transfer the dough to a greased bowl. Cover and leave to rise in a warm place for 1–1¼ hours until doubled in size.

5 Preheat a large baking sheet on the top shelf of the oven at 220°C (200°C fan oven) mark 7. Punch the dough to knock back, then divide in half. Shape each portion into a small, flattish round and put on a well-floured baking sheet. Cover loosely and leave to rise for a further 30 minutes.

6 Using a sharp knife, cut several slashes on each round, brush with a little milk and transfer to the heated baking sheet. Bake for 15 minutes, then lower the oven temperature to 190°C (170°C fan oven) mark 5 and bake for a further 15–20 minutes until the bread is risen and sounds hollow when tapped underneath. Cool on a wire rack.

A LITTLE EFFORT		NUTRITIONAL INFORMATION		Makes
Preparation Time 25 minutes, plus rising	**Cooking Time** 30–35 minutes, plus cooling	**Per Serving, based on 12 slices per loaf** 94 calories, 3g fat (of which 1g saturates), 14g carbohydrate, 0g salt	Vegetarian	**2** loaves

2

Soups, Salads and Quick Bites

Freezing tip

Freeze the soup at step 3 for up to one month.
To use Thaw overnight in the fridge. Reheat gently
and simmer for 5 minutes.

Carrot and Sweet Potato Soup

1 tbsp olive oil

1 large onion, chopped

1 tbsp coriander seeds

900g (2lb) carrots, roughly chopped

2 medium sweet potatoes, roughly chopped

2 litres (3½ pints) hot vegetable or chicken stock

2 tbsp white wine vinegar

2 tbsp freshly chopped coriander,
plus extra fresh sprigs to garnish

4 tbsp half-fat crème fraîche

salt and ground black pepper

1 Heat the oil in a large pan, add the onion and coriander seeds and cook over a medium heat for 5 minutes. Add the carrots and sweet potatoes and cook for a further 5 minutes.

2 Add the stock and bring the soup to the boil. Reduce the heat and leave to simmer for 25 minutes. Cool slightly, then put in a blender and whiz until slightly chunky. Add the vinegar and season with salt and pepper.

3 Cool half the quantity of soup, then freeze it. Pour the remainder into a clean pan, stir in the chopped coriander and reheat gently.

4 Divide the soup among four warmed bowls, then garnish each with 1 tbsp crème fraîche and fresh coriander sprigs to serve.

Serves 8	EASY		NUTRITIONAL INFORMATION	
	Preparation Time 15 minutes	**Cooking Time** 45 minutes	**Per Serving** 120 calories, 3g fat (of which 1g saturates), 22g carbohydrate, 0.7g salt	Vegetarian Gluten free

Special supper menu

▼ **Tomato, Pepper and Orange Soup**
▶ **Easy Chicken Casserole (see page 100)**
▶ **Chocolate Cherry Roll (see page 124)**

Tomato, Pepper and Orange Soup

leaves from 3 fresh rosemary sprigs

400g jar roasted red peppers, drained

2 tsp golden caster sugar

1 litre (1¾ pints) tomato juice

4 very ripe plum tomatoes

300ml (½ pint) hot chicken stock

450ml (¾ pint) freshly squeezed orange juice

ground black pepper

crusty bread to serve

1 Put the rosemary leaves into a food processor or blender, add the peppers, sugar, half the tomato juice and the plum tomatoes, and whiz together until slightly chunky.

2 Sieve the mixture into a pan and stir in the stock, orange juice and the remaining tomato juice. Bring to the boil and simmer gently for about 10 minutes. Season with plenty of pepper and serve with chunks of bread.

EASY		NUTRITIONAL INFORMATION		Serves
Preparation Time 15 minutes	**Cooking Time** 12 minutes	**Per Serving** 136 calories, 1g fat (of which trace saturates), 30g carbohydrate, 1.8g salt	Gluten free Dairy free	**4**

Spinach and Rice Soup

4 tbsp extra virgin olive oil

1 onion, finely chopped

2 garlic cloves, crushed

2 tsp freshly chopped thyme or
a large pinch of dried thyme

2 tsp freshly chopped rosemary
or a large pinch of dried rosemary

zest of ½ lemon

2 tsp ground coriander

¼ tsp cayenne pepper

125g (4oz) arborio (risotto) rice

1.1 litres (2 pints) vegetable stock

225g (8oz) fresh or frozen and thawed
spinach, shredded

4 tbsp pesto sauce

salt and ground black pepper

extra virgin olive oil and freshly
grated Parmesan to serve

1 Heat half the oil in a pan. Add the onion, garlic, herbs, lemon zest and spices, then fry gently for 5 minutes.

2 Add the remaining oil with the rice and cook, stirring, for 1 minute. Add the stock, bring to the boil and simmer gently for 20 minutes or until the rice is tender.

3 Stir the spinach into the soup with the pesto sauce. Cook for 2 minutes, then season to taste with salt and pepper.

4 Serve drizzled with a little oil and topped with Parmesan.

- ▶ Start the day: **Mango and Oat Smoothie (see page 32)**
- ▲ Lunch: **Spinach and Rice Soup**
- ▶ Special supper: **Salmon with Roasted Vegetables (see page 96)**
- ▶ Pudding: **Baked Apricots with Almonds (see page 123)**

EASY		NUTRITIONAL INFORMATION		Serves
Preparation Time 10 minutes	**Cooking Time** 25-30 minutes	**Per Serving** 336 calories, 19g fat (of which 3g saturates), 33g carbohydrate, 1.4g salt	Vegetarian Gluten free	4

Try Something Different

Replace the smoked tofu with shredded leftover roast chicken and simmer for 2–3 minutes.

Full-of-goodness Broth

1–2 tbsp medium curry paste

200ml (7fl oz) reduced-fat coconut milk

600ml (1 pint) hot vegetable stock

200g (7oz) smoked tofu, cubed

2 pak choi, chopped

a handful of sugarsnap peas

4 spring onions, chopped

lime to serve

1 Heat the curry paste in a pan for 1–2 minutes. Add the coconut milk and hot vegetable stock.

2 Bring to the boil, then add the smoked tofu, pak choi, sugarsnap peas and spring onions. Simmer for 1–2 minutes. Divide among four bowls and serve with a squeeze of lime.

Serves	EASY		NUTRITIONAL INFORMATION	
4	**Preparation Time** 10 minutes	**Cooking Time** 6-8 minutes	**Per Serving** 107 calories, 4g fat (of which trace saturates), 9g carbohydrate, 1g salt	Vegetarian Gluten free • Dairy free

Teriyaki Tuna with Noodle Broth

2 tbsp teriyaki marinade
juice of ½ lime
1 tbsp sweet chilli sauce
1 tbsp honey
4 tuna steaks, 125g (4oz) each
750ml (1¼ pints) hot vegetable stock
2 tbsp dry sherry
200g (7oz) medium egg noodles
200g (7oz) pak choi, roughly chopped
2 carrots, cut into matchsticks
250g (9oz) button mushrooms, sliced
freshly chopped coriander (optional)

1 Mix together the teriyaki marinade, lime juice, chilli sauce and honey in a large, shallow dish. Add the tuna and toss to coat.

2 Put the hot vegetable stock and sherry into a pan and bring to the boil. Add the noodles and cook for 4–5 minutes, then stir in the pak choi, carrots and mushrooms. Simmer for 1 minute.

3 Meanwhile, heat a frying pan until hot. Fry the tuna in the marinade for 2 minutes on each side until just cooked and still slightly pink inside. Cut into thick slices.

4 When the noodles are cooked, divide among four wide bowls, spoon the broth over them, then top each with the tuna and a sprinkling of coriander, if you like.

EASY		NUTRITIONAL INFORMATION		Serves
Preparation Time 10 minutes	**Cooking Time** 10 minutes	**Per Serving** 411 calories, 11g fat (of which 3g saturates), 43g carbohydrate, 0.6g salt	Dairy free	**4**

Cook's Tip

Chillies vary enormously in strength, from quite mild to blisteringly hot, depending on the type of chilli and its ripeness. Taste a small piece first to check it's not too hot for you.

Be extremely careful when handling chillies not to touch or rub your eyes with your fingers, as they will sting. Wash knives immediately after handling chillies for the same reason. As a precaution, use rubber gloves when preparing them if you like.

Chicken and Bean Soup

1 tbsp olive oil

1 onion, finely chopped

4 celery sticks, chopped

1 red chilli, seeded and roughly chopped (see Cook's Tip)

2 skinless chicken breasts, cut into strips

1 litre (1³/₄ pints) hot chicken or vegetable stock

100g (3¹/₂oz) bulgur wheat

2 x 400g cans cannellini beans, drained

400g can chopped tomatoes

25g (1oz) flat-leafed parsley, roughly chopped

wholegrain bread and hummus to serve

1 Heat the oil in a large, heavy-based pan. Add the onion, celery and chilli, and cook over a low heat for 10 minutes or until softened. Add the chicken and stir-fry for 3–4 minutes until golden.

2 Add the stock to the pan and bring to a simmer. Stir in the bulgur wheat and simmer for 15 minutes. Stir in the cannellini beans and tomatoes, and return to a simmer. Sprinkle the chopped parsley over and ladle into bowls. Serve with wholegrain bread and hummus.

Serves 4	EASY		NUTRITIONAL INFORMATION	
	Preparation Time 10 minutes	**Cooking Time** 30 minutes	**Per Serving** 351 calories, 6g fat (of which 1g saturates), 48g carbohydrate, 2.7g salt	Dairy free

▶ Start the day: **Breakfast Bruschetta (see page 39)**
▼ Lunch: **Warm Tofu, Fennel and Bean Salad**
▶ Supper: **Spring Vegetable Stew (see page 70)**
▶ Pudding: **Oranges with Caramel Sauce (see page 117)**

Warm Tofu, Fennel and Bean Salad

1 tbsp olive oil, plus 1 tsp

1 red onion, finely sliced

1 fennel bulb, finely sliced

1 tbsp cider vinegar

400g can butter beans, drained and rinsed

2 tbsp freshly chopped flat-leafed parsley

200g (7oz) smoked tofu

1 Heat 1 tbsp olive oil in a large frying pan. Add the sliced red onion and fennel, and cook over a medium heat for 5–10 minutes. Add the cider vinegar and heat through for 2 minutes. Stir in the butter beans and parsley. Tip into a bowl.

2 Slice the tofu into eight lengthways. Add to the pan with the remaining olive oil. Cook for 2 minutes on each side or until golden. Divide the bean mixture among four plates and add two slices of tofu to each plate.

EASY		NUTRITIONAL INFORMATION		Serves
Preparation Time 10 minutes	**Cooking Time** 15 minutes	**Per Serving** 150 calories, 6g fat (of which 1g saturates), 15g carbohydrate, 0.8g salt	Vegetarian Gluten free • Dairy free	**4**

Sprouted Bean and Mango Salad

3 tbsp mango chutney

grated zest and juice of 1 lime

2 tbsp olive oil

4 plum tomatoes

1 small red onion, finely chopped

1 red pepper, seeded and finely diced

1 yellow pepper, seeded and finely diced

1 mango, finely diced

4 tbsp freshly chopped coriander

150g (5oz) sprouted beans (see page 21)

salt and ground black pepper

1 To make the dressing, place the mango chutney in a small bowl and add the lime zest and juice. Whisk in the oil and season.

2 Quarter the tomatoes, discard the seeds and then dice. Put into a large bowl with the onion, peppers, mango, coriander and sprouted beans. Pour the dressing over and mix well. Serve the salad immediately.

Try Something Different

Use papaya instead of mango.

Ginger and chilli dressing Mix together 2 tsp grated fresh root ginger, 1 tbsp sweet chilli sauce, 2 tsp white wine vinegar and 2 tbsp walnut oil. Season with salt.

Peanut dressing Mix together 1 tbsp peanut butter, $1/4$ crushed dried chilli, 4 tsp white wine vinegar, 3 tbsp walnut oil, 1 tsp sesame oil and a dash of soy sauce.

EASY	NUTRITIONAL INFORMATION		Serves
Preparation Time 15 minutes	**Per Serving** 103 calories, 4g fat (of which 1g saturates), 15g carbohydrate, 0.1g salt	Vegetarian Gluten free • Dairy free	**6**

Warm Lentil and Egg Salad

1 tbsp olive oil

1 onion, 1 carrot and 1 celery stick, finely chopped

2 red peppers, seeded and roughly chopped

200g (7oz) flat mushrooms, sliced

200g (7oz) lentils, rinsed and drained

600ml (1 pint) hot vegetable stock

4 medium eggs

100g (3½ oz) baby leaf spinach

2 tbsp balsamic vinegar

ground black pepper

1 Heat the oil in a large pan. Add the onion, carrot and celery, and cook for 5 minutes. Add the peppers and mushrooms. Cover and cook for a further 5 minutes. Stir in the lentils and stock. Bring to the boil and simmer, covered, for 25–30 minutes.

2 Meanwhile, bring a large pan of water to the boil. Break the eggs into the water and cook for 3–4 minutes. Lift them out with a slotted spoon, drain on kitchen paper and keep warm.

3 A couple of minutes before the end of the lentil cooking time, add the spinach and cook until wilted. Stir in the vinegar. Spoon on to four plates or bowls and top each with a poached egg. Season with pepper and serve.

Serves 4	EASY		NUTRITIONAL INFORMATION	
	Preparation Time 15 minutes	**Cooking Time** 35-40 minutes	**Per Serving** 317 calories, 10g fat (of which 2g saturates), 37g carbohydrate, 0.7g salt	Vegetarian Gluten free • Dairy free

Cook's Tip

Buy tuna steak canned in extra virgin olive oil, which flakes easily into large, meaty flakes and has a good flavour.

Tuna, Bean and Red Onion Salad

400g can cannellini beans, drained and rinsed

1 small red onion, very finely sliced

1 tbsp red wine vinegar

225g can tuna steak in oil (see Cook's Tip)

2 tbsp freshly chopped parsley

salt and ground black pepper

1 Put the cannellini beans, onion slices and wine vinegar into a bowl, season with a little salt and mix well. Add the tuna with its oil, breaking the fish into large flakes.

2 Add half the chopped parsley and season generously with pepper. Toss the salad, then scatter the remaining parsley over the top. Serve with a green salad and plenty of warm crusty bread.

EASY	NUTRITIONAL INFORMATION		Serves
Preparation Time 5 minutes	**Per Serving** 190 calories, 6g fat (of which 1g saturates), 15g carbohydrate, 1.1g salt	Vegetarian Gluten free • Dairy free	**4**

Warm Lentil, Chicken and Broccoli Salad

125g (4oz) Puy lentils

225g (8oz) broccoli, cut into small florets

1 large garlic clove

1 tsp sea salt

1 tsp English mustard powder

2 tbsp balsamic vinegar

4 tbsp olive oil

1 red onion, thinly sliced

175g (6oz) back bacon, roughly chopped

350g (12oz) smoked chicken breast, roughly chopped

salt and ground black pepper

1 Cook the lentils in plenty of unsalted water for about 35 minutes or until soft.

2 Meanwhile, blanch the broccoli in a pan of boiling salted water for 2 minutes, drain and plunge into a bowl of icy cold water. When cold, drain well and set aside.

3 Using a pestle and mortar, or a heavy bowl and the end of a rolling pin, pound the garlic and sea salt together until creamy, add the mustard and continue mixing. Whisk in the vinegar, then 3 tbsp olive oil and set the dressing to one side.

4 Heat the remaining oil in a frying pan, add the onion and bacon, and cook over a medium heat for 5 minutes or until the onion is beginning to soften and the bacon is crisp. Add the chicken and broccoli, and stir fry for 1–2 minutes.

5 Drain the lentils, add the broccoli mixture and toss with the dressing. Season to taste and serve warm.

Try Something Different

For an even quicker supper, use a can of Puy lentils – just turn out into a saucepan, heat and drain. Proceed with step 5.

Serves	EASY		NUTRITIONAL INFORMATION	
4	**Preparation Time** 15 minutes	**Cooking Time** 35 minutes	**Per Serving** 405 calories, 21g fat (of which 5g saturates), 17g carbohydrate, 3.1g salt	Gluten free Dairy free

Chicken with Bulgur Wheat Salad

zest and juice of 1 lemon

4 skinless chicken breasts, slashed several times

1 tbsp ground coriander

2 tsp olive oil

salt and ground black pepper

For the salad

225g (8oz) bulgur wheat

6 tomatoes, chopped

½ cucumber, chopped

4 spring onions, chopped

50g (2oz) dried dates, chopped

50g (2oz) almonds, chopped

3 tbsp freshly chopped flat-leafed parsley

3 tbsp freshly chopped mint

1 Put half the lemon zest and juice into a medium-sized bowl, then add the chicken breasts, coriander and 1 tsp oil. Toss well to mix. Leave to marinate while you prepare the salad.

2 Meanwhile, cook the bulgur wheat according to the packet instructions (about 10 minutes). Put into a bowl, add the remaining salad ingredients and season well. Add the remaining lemon zest, juice and oil. Stir well.

3 Preheat the grill to high and cook the chicken for 10 minutes on each side or until cooked through. The juices should run clear when the meat is pierced with a sharp knife. Slice the chicken and serve with the salad.

Serves 4	EASY		NUTRITIONAL INFORMATION	
	Preparation Time 20 minutes, plus marinating	**Cooking Time** 30 minutes	**Per Serving** 429 calories, 12g fat (of which 1g saturates), 45g carbohydrate, 0.2g salt	Dairy free

Try Something Different

Use mixed beans, chickpeas or red kidney beans instead of cannellini beans.
Replace the turkey with cooked chicken.

2 tbsp fresh tarragon, roughly chopped

2 tbsp flat-leafed parsley, roughly chopped

1 tbsp olive oil

2 tbsp crème fraîche

200ml (7fl oz) mayonnaise

juice of ½ lemon

450g (1lb) cooked turkey, cut into bite-sized pieces

400g can cannellini beans, rinsed and drained

50g (2oz) sunblush or sun-dried tomatoes

salt and ground black pepper

finely sliced spring onion to garnish

For the shallot dressing

2 tbsp sunflower oil

1 tsp walnut oil

2 tsp red wine vinegar

1 small shallot, very finely chopped

pinch of caster sugar

Tarragon Turkey and Bean Salad

1 Put the herbs in a food processor and add the olive oil. Whiz until the herbs are chopped. Add the crème fraîche, mayonnaise and lemon juice to the processor and season, then whiz until well combined. Alternatively, chop the herbs by hand, mix with the olive oil, then beat in the crème fraîche, mayonnaise, lemon juice and seasoning. Toss the turkey with the herb dressing in a large bowl and put to one side.

2 To make the shallot dressing, whisk the ingredients together in a small bowl and season with salt and pepper.

3 Tip the cannellini beans into a bowl, toss with the shallot dressing and season well. Arrange the cannellini beans on a serving dish. Roughly chop the tomatoes. Top the beans with the dressed turkey and tomatoes, and garnish with spring onion.

EASY	NUTRITIONAL INFORMATION		Serves
Preparation Time 15–20 minutes	**Per Serving** 767 calories, 58g fat (of which 11g saturates), 17g carbohydrate, 1.6g salt	Gluten free	**4**

Try Something Different

For a vegetarian alternative, replace the ham with 150g (5oz) cubed Gruyère, or Cheddar cheese.

Spicy cumin dressing: mix together 2 tbsp red wine vinegar, 1 tsp ground cumin, a pinch of caster sugar and 5 tbsp olive oil. Season to taste.

Balsamic dressing: mix together 3 tbsp balsamic vinegar, 2 tbsp olive oil and 2 tsp wholegrain mustard.

Apple, Celery, Ham and Pecan Salad

450g (1lb) fennel, halved

2 large Braeburn or Cox's apples, about 450g (1lb), quartered, cored and sliced

75g (3oz) shelled pecan nuts

300g (11oz) cooked ham, cut into wide strips

1 head chicory, divided into leaves

fresh flat-leafed parsley sprigs to garnish

For the poppy seed dressing

1 tsp clear honey

2 tsp German or Dijon mustard

3 tbsp cider vinegar

9 tbsp vegetable oil

2 tsp poppy seeds

salt and ground black pepper

1 To make the dressing, whisk together the honey, mustard, vinegar and seasoning in a small bowl. Whisk in the vegetable oil, then the poppy seeds. Set to one side.

2 Remove the centre core from the fennel and slice thinly lengthways. Place the fennel, apples, nuts, ham and chicory in a large serving bowl. Toss with the dressing and adjust the seasoning if necessary. Garnish with parsley sprigs and serve immediately.

Serves 6	EASY		NUTRITIONAL INFORMATION	
	Preparation Time 10 minutes		**Per Serving** 340 calories, 28g fat (of which 3g saturates), 10g carbohydrate, 1.6g salt	Gluten free Dairy free

Cook's Tip

Sunblush tomatoes are partly dried, but are not as dehydrated as sun-dried tomatoes.

Chilli Beef Noodle Salad

150g (5oz) dried rice noodles

juice of 1 lime

1 lemongrass stalk, outside leaves discarded, finely chopped

1 red chilli, seeded and chopped (see page 50)

2 tsp finely chopped fresh root ginger

2 garlic cloves, crushed

1 tbsp Thai fish sauce

3 tbsp extra virgin olive oil

50g (2oz) rocket

125g (4oz) sliced cold roast beef

125g (4oz) sunblush tomatoes, chopped

salt and ground black pepper

1 Put the noodles in a large bowl and pour over boiling water to cover. Put to one side for 15 minutes.

2 Meanwhile, in a small bowl, whisk together the lime juice, lemongrass, chilli, ginger, garlic, fish sauce and oil. Season.

3 While they are still warm, drain the noodles well, put in a large bowl and toss with the dressing. Allow to cool.

4 Just before serving, toss the rocket leaves, sliced beef and chopped tomatoes through the noodles.

EASY	NUTRITIONAL INFORMATION		Serves
Preparation Time 15 minutes, plus 15 minutes soaking	**Per Serving** 286 calories, 11g fat (of which 2g saturates), 33g carbohydrate, 0.8g salt	Gluten free Dairy free	**4**

Spring Lamb and Flageolet Bean Salad

2–3 lamb fillets, about 700g (1½lb) in total

1 tbsp Dijon mustard

5 tbsp olive oil

1 tsp freshly chopped parsley

2 garlic cloves

juice of 1 lemon

400g can flageolet or cannellini beans, drained and rinsed

125g (4oz) frisée lettuce or curly endive

250g (9oz) baby plum or cherry tomatoes, halved

salt and ground black pepper

1 Rub the lamb fillets with the mustard and season with pepper. Place 1 tbsp olive oil in a non-stick frying pan and fry the lamb over a medium heat for 5–7 minutes on each side for medium rare, 8–10 minutes for well done. Remove the lamb, cover and set aside for 5 minutes. This allows the meat to relax, which makes slicing easier.

2 To make the dressing, place the parsley, garlic, lemon juice and remaining olive oil in a food processor and process for 10 seconds. (Alternatively, put the ingredients into a screw-topped jar and shake to combine.)

3 Place the beans, frisée or curly endive and the tomatoes in a bowl, combine with the dressing and season to taste.

4 Slice the lamb into 1cm (½ in) slices and place on top of the flageolet salad. Serve immediately.

Try Something Different

- -

For a vegetarian alternative, skewer the whole tomatoes on soaked wooden kebab sticks, alternating with small mozzarella balls. Grill the kebabs and drizzle with 2 tbsp pesto sauce thinned with a little olive oil.

EASY		NUTRITIONAL INFORMATION		Serves
Preparation Time 5 minutes	**Cooking Time** 10–20 minutes, plus 5 minutes resting	**Per Serving** 535 calories, 35g fat (of which 11g saturates), 17g carbohydrate, 1.4g salt	Gluten free Dairy free	**4**

3

Midweek Suppers

Cook's Tip

Bulgur wheat is widely used in Middle Eastern cooking and has a light, nutty flavour and texture. It is available in several different sizes – from coarse to fine.

Roasted Tomato Bulgur Salad

175g (6oz) bulgur wheat

700g (1½ lb) cherry tomatoes or baby plum tomatoes

8 tbsp extra virgin olive oil

a handful each of mint and basil, roughly chopped, plus fresh basil sprigs to garnish

3–4 tbsp balsamic vinegar

1 bunch spring onions, sliced

salt and ground black pepper

1 Put the bulgur wheat in a bowl and add boiling water to cover by 1cm (½ in). Leave to soak for 30 minutes.

2 Preheat the oven to 220°C (200°C fan oven) mark 7. Put the tomatoes in a small roasting tin, drizzle with half the oil and add half the mint. Season with salt and pepper, and roast for 10–15 minutes until beginning to soften.

3 Put the remaining oil and the vinegar into a large bowl. Add the warm pan juices from the roasted tomatoes and the soaked bulgur wheat.

4 Stir in the remaining chopped herbs and the spring onions, and check the seasoning. You may need a little more vinegar depending on the sweetness of the tomatoes.

5 Carefully toss in the tomatoes and serve garnished with basil sprigs.

Serves	EASY		NUTRITIONAL INFORMATION	
6	**Preparation Time** 10 minutes, plus 30 minutes soaking	**Cooking Time** 10–15 minutes	**Per Serving** 225 calories, 15g fat (of which 2g saturates), 19g carbohydrate, 0g salt	Vegetarian Dairy free

Cook's Tip

Tamarind paste has a very sharp, sour flavour and is widely used in Asian and South-east Asian cooking.

2 tbsp vegetable oil

2 onions, finely sliced

2 garlic cloves, crushed

1 tbsp ground coriander

1 tsp mild chilli powder

1 tbsp black mustard seeds

2 tbsp tamarind paste

2 tbsp sun-dried tomato paste

750g (1lb 10oz) new potatoes, quartered

400g can chopped tomatoes

1 litre (1¾ pints) hot vegetable stock

250g (9oz) green beans, trimmed

2 x 400g cans chickpeas, drained and rinsed

2 tsp garam masala

salt and ground black pepper

Chickpea Curry

1 Heat the oil in a pan and fry the onions for 10–15 minutes until golden – when they have a good colour they will add depth of flavour. Add the garlic, coriander, chilli, mustard seeds, tamarind paste and sun-dried tomato paste. Cook for 1–2 minutes until the aroma from the spices is released.

2 Add the potatoes and toss in the spices for 1–2 minutes. Add the tomatoes and stock, and season with salt and pepper. Cover and bring to the boil. Simmer, half covered, for 20 minutes or until the potatoes are just cooked.

3 Add the beans and chickpeas, and continue to cook for 5 minutes or until the beans are tender and the chickpeas are warmed through. Stir in the garam masala and serve.

EASY		NUTRITIONAL INFORMATION		Serves
Preparation Time 20 minutes	**Cooking Time** 40-45 minutes	**Per Serving** 291 calories, 8g fat (of which 1g saturates), 46g carbohydrate, 1.3g salt	Vegetarian Gluten free • Dairy free	**6**

Spicy Bean and Tomato Fajitas

2 tbsp sunflower oil

1 onion, sliced

2 garlic cloves, crushed

½ tsp hot chilli powder

1 tsp ground coriander

1 tsp ground cumin

1 tbsp tomato purée

400g can chopped tomatoes

225g can red kidney beans, drained and rinsed

300g can borlotti beans, drained and rinsed

300g can flageolet beans, drained and rinsed

150ml (¼ pint) hot vegetable stock

2 ripe avocados, quartered and chopped

juice of ½ lime

1 tbsp freshly chopped coriander, plus extra sprigs to garnish

6 ready-made flour tortillas

150ml (5 fl oz) soured cream

salt and ground black pepper

lime wedges to serve

1 Heat the oil in a large pan. Add the onion and cook gently for 5 minutes. Add the garlic and spices and cook for a further 2 minutes.

2 Add the tomato purée and cook for 1 minute, then add the tomatoes, beans and hot stock. Season well with salt and pepper, bring to the boil and simmer for 15 minutes, stirring occasionally.

3 Put the avocado into a bowl, add the lime juice and the chopped coriander, and mash together. Season to taste.

4 To warm the tortillas either wrap them in foil and heat in the oven at 180°C (160°C fan oven) mark 4 for 10 minutes, or put on a plate and microwave on full power for 45 seconds.

5 Spoon the beans down the centre of each tortilla. Add a little avocado and soured cream, then fold the two sides in so that they overlap. Garnish with coriander sprigs and serve with lime wedges.

EASY		NUTRITIONAL INFORMATION		Serves
Preparation Time 15 minutes	**Cooking Time** 25 minutes	**Per Serving** 508 calories, 20g fat (of which 6g saturates), 71g carbohydrate, 1.6g salt	Vegetarian	**6**

Spring Vegetable Stew

225g (8oz) new potatoes, scrubbed

75g (3oz) unsalted butter

4 shallots, blanched in boiling water, drained, peeled and thinly sliced

1 garlic clove, crushed

2 tsp freshly chopped thyme

1 tsp grated lime zest

6 baby leeks, trimmed and sliced into 5cm (2in) lengths

125g (4oz) baby carrots, scrubbed

125g (4oz) podded peas

125g (4oz) podded broad beans

300ml (½ pint) vegetable stock

1 Little Gem lettuce, shredded

4 tbsp freshly chopped herbs, such as chervil, chives, mint and parsley

salt and ground black pepper

1 Put the potatoes in a pan of lightly salted water. Bring to the boil, cover and par-boil for 5 minutes. Drain and refresh under cold water.

2 Meanwhile, melt half the butter in a large sauté pan, add the shallots, garlic, thyme and lime zest, and fry gently for 5 minutes or until softened and lightly golden. Add the leeks and carrots and sauté for a further 5 minutes. Stir in the potatoes, peas and broad beans, then pour in the stock and bring to the boil. Cover the pan, reduce the heat and simmer gently for 10 minutes. Remove the lid and cook, uncovered, for a further 5–8 minutes until all the vegetables are tender.

3 Add the shredded lettuce to the stew with the chopped herbs and remaining butter. Heat through until the butter is melted. Check the seasoning and serve at once.

Serves	EASY		NUTRITIONAL INFORMATION	
4	**Preparation Time** 20 minutes	**Cooking Time** 30–35 minutes	**Per Serving** 270 calories, 17g fat (of which 10g saturates), 23g carbohydrate, 0.6g salt	Vegetarian Gluten free • Dairy free

300g (11oz) conchiglie pasta

30g can anchovies, drained and chopped, oil from the can put to one side

400g can borlotti beans, drained and rinsed

a handful of spinach leaves

For the tomato sauce

2 tbsp oil from the drained anchovies

2 carrots, diced

1 large onion, diced

2 celery sticks, diced

1 bay leaf

250ml (9fl oz) dry white wine

300ml (½ pint) hot vegetable stock

2 x 400g cans chopped tomatoes

1 tsp caster sugar or to taste

salt and ground black pepper

Borlotti, Anchovy and Spinach Pasta

1 To make the tomato sauce, preheat the oven to 180°C (160°C fan oven) mark 4. Heat the oil in a flameproof casserole on the hob. Add the carrots, onion, celery and bay leaf, and season to taste. Cook gently for 15–20 minutes, stirring occasionally, until soft and golden.

2 Add the wine, stock and tomatoes. Bring to the boil, then cover and cook in the oven for 20 minutes. Remove the lid and cook for a further 20 minutes until the sauce is thick. Taste the sauce – if it's a little acidic, add the caster sugar.

3 Cook the pasta in a large pan of boiling salted water according to the packet instructions. Add the anchovies to the simmering tomato sauce with 1 tbsp of the oil from the can, the beans and spinach. Heat for 5 minutes. Drain the pasta and toss through the sauce. Serve.

Serves 4	EASY		NUTRITIONAL INFORMATION	
	Preparation Time 10 minutes	**Cooking Time** 1 hour	**Per Serving** 518 calories, 9g fat (of which 1g saturates), 86g carbohydrate, 1.8g salt	Dairy free

Cook's Tip

To make spring onion curls, thinly slice the onions lengthways, soak in ice-cold water for 30 minutes, then drain well.

Seafood and Lime Kebabs

225g (8oz) peeled raw king prawns, deveined

550g (1¼lb) monkfish fillet, cut into 2.5cm (1in) cubes

juice of ½ lime

1 garlic clove, crushed

2 tbsp chilli oil

2 tbsp teriyaki sauce

2 limes and 1 lemon, each cut into 8 wedges

finely chopped and seeded green chilli (see page 50), spring onion curls (see Cook's Tip) and flat-leafed parsley to garnish

rice to serve

1 Put the king prawns and monkfish in a bowl. Combine the lime juice, garlic, chilli oil and teriyaki sauce and pour over the top. Stir well to coat and leave in a cool place for up to 1 hour. Meanwhile, if using wooden skewers, soak eight in water for 30 minutes.

2 Remove the seafood from the marinade and thread on to the skewers interspersed with lime and lemon wedges.

3 Heat a griddle or grill. Grill the kebabs for 3 minutes, turning once during cooking and brushing with the marinade. Garnish with green chilli, spring onions and parsley, and serve with rice.

EASY		NUTRITIONAL INFORMATION		Serves
Preparation Time 20 minutes, plus 1 hour marinating	**Cooking Time** 3 minutes	**Per Serving** 184 calories, 6g fat (of which 1g saturates), trace carbohydrate, 0.8g salt	Gluten free Dairy free	**4**

Cook's Tip

There's no need to turn the salmon over halfway through – just remember to keep a close eye on it and lower the heat if necessary, so that the honey in the sauce doesn't burn.

Dill Salmon

4 tbsp Dijon mustard-flavoured mayonnaise

4 tbsp finely chopped fresh dill

4 tbsp clear honey

1 tbsp lemon juice

4 thick skinless salmon fillets, about 150g (5oz) each

tomato salad to serve

1 Preheat the grill to high. Put the mayonnaise into a bowl with the dill, honey and lemon juice. Mix together.

2 Put the salmon fillets on to a baking sheet and spread the mayonnaise mixture over the top. Grill for 5–7 minutes, depending on the thickness, until just cooked. Serve with tomato salad.

Serves 4	EASY		NUTRITIONAL INFORMATION	
	Preparation Time 2 minutes	**Cooking Time** 5-7 minutes	**Per Serving** 421 calories, 28g fat (of which 5g saturates), 12g carbohydrate, 0.4g salt	Gluten free Dairy free

▶ Start the day: **Beans on Toast**
(see page 40)
▶ Lunch: **Carrot and Sweet Potato Soup**
(see page 44)
▼ Supper: **Baked Fish**
▶ Pudding: **Summer Fruit Compote**
(see page 110)

1 small butternut squash, peeled and cut into small cubes

½ red onion, finely sliced

2 garlic cloves, finely chopped

1 tbsp roughly chopped dill, plus extra sprigs to garnish

1 tbsp olive oil

4 thick haddock or salmon fillets, about 150g (5oz) each

125g (4oz) fresh spinach

salt and ground black pepper

lemon wedges and boiled new potatoes to serve

Baked Fish

1 Preheat the oven to 220°C (200°C fan) mark 7. Cut out four 40.5cm (16in) squares of foil.

2 Put the squash in a bowl. Add the onion, garlic, dill and oil, and toss to coat. Season well with salt and pepper. Divide the vegetable mixture equally among the four squares of foil.

3 Top each pile of vegetables with a piece of fish. Season again, then bring the foil together and crimp the edges so that the fish and vegetables are completely enclosed. Put the parcels on a baking tray and roast for 15 minutes or until the fish is cooked through and the squash is just tender.

4 Carefully open each of the foil parcels and add the spinach. Close again and roast for a further 5 minutes or until the spinach has wilted. Garnish with dill and serve with lemon wedges to squeeze over the fish, and new potatoes.

EASY		NUTRITIONAL INFORMATION		Serves
Preparation Time 10 minutes	**Cooking Time** 20 minutes	**Per Serving** 191 calories, 4g fat (of which 1g saturates), 7g carbohydrate, 0.4g salt	Gluten free Dairy free	**4**

Cook's Tip

Basmati rice is prized for its delicate fragrant flavour. Its long grains are firm and separate when cooked, not sticky, making it perfect for this tasty kedgeree.

Salmon and Coriander Kedgeree

1 tbsp olive oil

4 shallots, chopped

225g (8oz) basmati rice

450ml (¾ pint) hot fish stock

100g (3½ oz) frozen peas

300g (11oz) hot-smoked salmon flakes

a handful of freshly chopped coriander

salt and ground black pepper

lime wedges to serve

1 Heat the oil in a large pan over a low heat and fry the shallots for 5 minutes or until soft. Add the rice and stir to mix everything together. Pour in the stock. Cover and cook for 10 minutes over a low heat until the rice is almost cooked and most of the liquid has been absorbed.

2 Add the peas and salmon and cook, uncovered, for 2–3 minutes until the peas are tender. Season with salt and pepper, scatter over the chopped coriander and serve with lime wedges to squeeze over.

Serves 4	EASY		NUTRITIONAL INFORMATION	
	Preparation Time 5 minutes	**Cooking Time** 20 minutes	**Per Serving** 368 calories, 7g fat (of which 1g saturates), 50g carbohydrate, 3.8g salt	Gluten free Dairy free

Cook's Tip

Toasting the cashew nuts in a dry frying pan before adding them to the salad brings out their flavour, giving them an intense, nutty taste and a wonderful golden colour.

Orange and Chicken Salad

50g (2oz) cashew nuts

zest and juice of 2 oranges

2 tbsp marmalade

1 tbsp honey

1 tbsp oyster sauce

400g (14oz) roast chicken, shredded

a handful of chopped raw vegetables, such as cucumber, carrot, red and yellow pepper and Chinese leaves

1 Put the cashew nuts in a frying pan and cook for 2–3 minutes until golden. Tip into a large serving bowl.

2 To make the dressing, put the orange zest and juice into the frying pan with the marmalade, honey and oyster sauce. Bring to the boil, stirring, then simmer for 2–3 minutes until slightly thickened.

3 Add the roast chicken to the serving bowl with the chopped raw vegetables. Pour the dressing over the salad, toss everything together and serve immediately.

EASY		NUTRITIONAL INFORMATION		Serves
Preparation Time 15 minutes	**Cooking Time** 10 minutes	**Per Serving** 252 calories, 8g fat (of which 2g saturates), 20g carbohydrate, 0.5g salt	Gluten free Dairy free	**4**

▶ Start the day: **Energy-boosting Muesli (see page 37)**

▶ Lunch: **Apple, Celery, Ham and Pecan Salad (see page 60)**

▼ Supper: **Grilled Chicken with Mango Salsa**

▶ Pudding: **Spiced Winter Fruit (see page 120)**

Grilled Chicken with Mango Salsa

4 chicken breasts

juice of ½ lime

oil-water spray

salt and ground black pepper

rocket leaves to serve

For the salsa

1 mango, peeled, stoned and diced

1 small head of fennel, trimmed and diced

1 fresh chilli, seeded and finely diced (see page 50)

1 tbsp balsamic vinegar

juice of ½ lime

2 tbsp freshly chopped flat-leafed parsley

2 tbsp freshly chopped mint

1 Put the chicken on a grill pan and season generously with salt and pepper. Pour over the lime juice and spray with the oil-water. Grill for 8–10 minutes on each side until cooked through and the juices run clear when pierced with a skewer. Set aside.

2 Combine all the salsa ingredients in a bowl and season generously with salt and pepper. Spoon alongside the chicken and serve with rocket leaves.

Serves 4	EASY		NUTRITIONAL INFORMATION	
	Preparation Time 10 minutes	**Cooking Time** 20 minutes	**Per Serving** 288 calories, 14g fat (of which 4g saturates), 7g carbohydrate, 0.2g salt	Gluten free Dairy free

Try Something Different

Use flageolet beans or other canned beans instead of mixed beans and garnish with fresh basil or oregano.

One-pan Chicken with Tomatoes

4 chicken thighs

1 red onion, sliced

400g can chopped tomatoes with herbs

400g can mixed beans

2 tsp balsamic vinegar

freshly chopped flat-leafed parsley to garnish

1 Heat a non-stick pan and fry the chicken thighs, skin side down, until golden. Turn over and fry for 5 minutes.

2 Add the red onion and fry for 5 minutes. Add the tomatoes, mixed beans and balsamic vinegar. Cover and simmer for 10–12 minutes until piping hot. Garnish with parsley and serve immediately.

EASY		NUTRITIONAL INFORMATION		Serves
Preparation Time 5 minutes	**Cooking Time** 20-25 minutes	**Per Serving** 238 calories, 4g fat (of which 1g saturates), 20g carbohydrate, 1g salt	Gluten free Dairy free	**4**

Pork and Noodle Stir-fry

1 tbsp sesame oil

5cm (2in) piece fresh root ginger, peeled and grated

2 tbsp soy sauce

1 tbsp fish sauce

½ red chilli, finely chopped (see page 50)

450g (1lb) stir-fry pork strips

2 red peppers, halved, seeded and roughly chopped

250g (9oz) baby sweetcorn, halved lengthways

200g (7oz) sugarsnap peas, halved

300g (11oz) bean sprouts

250g (9oz) rice noodles

1 Put the oil into a large bowl. Add the ginger, soy sauce, fish sauce, chilli and pork strips. Mix well and leave to marinate for 10 minutes.

2 Heat a large wok until hot. Lift the pork out of the marinade with a slotted spoon and add to the pan. Stir-fry over a high heat for 5 minutes. Add the red peppers, corn, sugarsnap peas, bean sprouts and remaining marinade, and stir-fry for a further 2–3 minutes until the pork is cooked.

3 Meanwhile, bring a large pan of water to the boil and cook the noodles according to the packet instructions.

4 Drain the noodles, tip into the wok and toss together, then serve immediately.

Try Something Different

Use 450g (1lb) chicken or turkey strips instead of pork.

Serves	EASY		NUTRITIONAL INFORMATION		
4	**Preparation Time** 10 minutes, plus 10 minutes marinating	**Cooking Time** 7-8 minutes	**Per Serving** 500 calories, 9g fat (of which 2g saturates), 67g carbohydrate, 3.4g salt		Gluten free Dairy free

Spiced Lamb with Lentils

1 tbsp sunflower oil
8 lamb chops, trimmed of all fat
2 onions, finely sliced
1 tsp paprika
1 tsp ground cinnamon
400g can lentils, drained
400g can chickpeas, drained
300ml (½ pint) lamb or chicken stock
salt and ground black pepper
freshly chopped flat-leafed parsley to garnish

1 Preheat the oven to 180°C (160°C fan oven) mark 4. Heat the oil in a large non-stick frying pan, add the chops and brown on both sides. Remove from the pan with a slotted spoon.

2 Add the onions, paprika and cinnamon. Fry for 2–3 minutes. Stir in the lentils and chickpeas. Season, then spoon into a shallow 2 litre (3½ pint) ovenproof dish.

3 Put the chops on top of the onion and lentil mixture and pour the stock over them.

4 Cover the dish tightly and cook in the oven for 1½ hours or until the chops are tender. Uncover and cook for 30 minutes or until lightly browned. Scatter over the parsley and serve hot.

Try Something Different

Replace the lamb chops with 4 chicken legs; cook for 30–35 minutes until cooked through. Uncover and cook for a further 15 minutes.

EASY		NUTRITIONAL INFORMATION		Serves
Preparation Time 10 minutes	**Cooking Time** 2¼ hours	**Per Serving** 315 calories, 12g fat (of which 2g saturates), 35g carbohydrate, 1g salt	Gluten free Dairy free	**4**

Sweet Chilli Beef Stir-fry

1 tsp chilli oil

1 tbsp soy sauce

1 tbsp clear honey

1 garlic clove, crushed

1 large red chilli, halved, seeded and chopped (see page 50)

400g (14oz) lean beef, cut into strips

1 tsp sunflower oil

1 broccoli head, sliced into small florets

200g (7oz) mangetouts, halved

1 red pepper, halved, seeded and cut into strips

1 Put the chilli oil in a medium-sized shallow bowl. Add the soy sauce, honey, garlic and chilli, and stir well. Add the strips of beef and toss in the marinade.

2 Heat the sunflower oil in a wok over a high heat until it is very hot. Cook the strips of beef in two batches, then remove them from the pan and set to one side and keep warm. Wipe the pan with kitchen paper to remove any residue.

3 Add the broccoli, mangetouts, red pepper and 2 tbsp water. Stir fry for 5–6 minutes until starting to soften. Return the beef to the pan to heat through.

Try Something Different

Other vegetables are just as good: try pak choi, baby sweetcorn, courgettes or carrots cut into thin strips.

Serves 4	EASY		NUTRITIONAL INFORMATION	
	Preparation Time 10 minutes	**Cooking Time** 15 minutes	**Per Serving** 273 calories, 13g fat (of which 5g saturates), 8g carbohydrate, 0.2g salt	Gluten free Dairy free

4

Special Suppers

Special supper menu

▼ **Asparagus and Quail's Egg Salad**
▶ **Cod with Oriental Vegetables**
   (see page 94)
▶ **Tropical Fruit Pots (see page 118)**

Asparagus and Quail's Egg Salad

24 quail's eggs
24 asparagus spears, trimmed
juice of ½ lemon
5 tbsp olive oil
4 large spring onions, finely sliced
100g (3½ oz) watercress, roughly chopped
a few fresh dill and tarragon sprigs
salt and ground black pepper

1 Add the quail's eggs to a pan of boiling water and cook for 2 minutes, then drain and plunge into cold water. Cook the asparagus in boiling salted water for 2 minutes or until just tender. Drain, plunge into cold water and leave to cool.

2 Whisk together the lemon juice, olive oil and seasoning. Stir in the spring onions and put to one side.

3 Peel the quail's eggs and cut in half. Put into a large bowl with the asparagus, watercress, dill and tarragon. Pour over the dressing and lightly toss all the ingredients together. Adjust the seasoning and serve.

Serves	EASY		NUTRITIONAL INFORMATION	
8	**Preparation Time** 30 minutes	**Cooking Time** 2 minutes	**Per Serving** 127 calories, 11g fat (of which 2g saturates), 1g carbohydrate, 0.1g salt	Vegetarian Gluten free • Dairy free

Try Something Different

Replace the goat's cheese with two roasted skinless shredded chicken breasts.

½ tbsp ground cumin

½ tsp ground cinnamon

2 tbsp sunflower oil

2 large red onions, sliced

250g (9oz) basmati rice

600ml (1 pint) hot vegetable or chicken stock

400g can lentils, drained and rinsed

For the salad

75g (3oz) watercress

250g (9oz) broccoli, steamed and chopped into 2.5cm (1in) pieces

25g (1oz) sultanas

75g (3oz) chopped dried apricots

75g (3oz) mixed nuts and seeds

2 tbsp freshly chopped flat-leafed parsley

100g (3½ oz) goat's cheese, crumbled

Warm Spiced Rice Salad

1 Put the cumin and cinnamon into a large, deep frying pan and heat gently for 1–2 minutes. Add the oil and onions, then fry over a low heat for 8–10 minutes until the onion is soft and golden. Add the rice, toss to coat in the spices and onions, then add the stock. Cover and cook for 12–15 minutes until the stock is absorbed and the rice is cooked. Season, tip into a serving bowl and add the lentils.

2 To make the salad, add the watercress, broccoli, sultanas, apricots, and mixed nuts and seeds to the bowl. Scatter over the parsley, then toss together, top with the cheese and serve immediately.

EASY		NUTRITIONAL INFORMATION		Serves
Preparation Time 10 minutes	**Cooking Time** 20–30 minutes	**Per Serving** 700 calories, 27g fat (of which 6g saturates), 88g carbohydrate, 0.7g salt	Vegetarian Gluten free	**4**

Pumpkin with Chickpeas

900g (2lb) pumpkin or squash, such as butternut, crown prince or kabocha (see Cook's Tip), peeled, seeded and chopped into roughly 2cm (³/₄ in) cubes

1 garlic clove, crushed

2 tbsp olive oil

2 x 400g cans chickpeas, drained

½ red onion, thinly sliced

1 large bunch coriander, roughly chopped

salt and ground black pepper

steamed spinach to serve

For the tahini sauce

1 large garlic clove, crushed

3 tbsp tahini paste

juice of 1 lemon

1 Preheat the oven to 220°C (200°C fan oven) mark 7. Toss the squash or pumpkin in the garlic and oil, and season. Put in a roasting tin and roast for 25 minutes or until soft.

2 Meanwhile, put the chickpeas in a pan with 150ml (¼ pint) water over a medium heat, to warm through.

3 To make the tahini sauce, put the garlic in a bowl, add a pinch of salt, then whisk in the tahini paste. Add the lemon juice and 4–5 tbsp cold water – enough to make a consistency somewhere between single and double cream – and season.

4 Drain the chickpeas, put in a large bowl, then add the pumpkin, onion and coriander. Pour on the tahini sauce and toss carefully. Adjust the seasoning and serve while warm, with spinach.

Cook's Tip

Kabocha is a Japanese variety of winter squash, and has a dull-coloured deep green skin with whitish stripes. Its flesh is an intense yellow-orange colour.

EASY		NUTRITIONAL INFORMATION		Serves
Preparation Time 15 minutes	**Cooking Time** 25-30 minutes	**Per Serving** 228 calories, 12g fat (of which 2g saturates), 22g carbohydrate, 0.6g salt	Vegetarian Gluten free • Dairy free	**6**

Try Something Different

Replace carrots and/or broccoli with alternative vegetables – try baby sweetcorn, sugarsnap peas or mangetouts and simmer for only 5 minutes until tender.

2–3 tbsp red Thai curry paste

2.5cm (1in) piece fresh root ginger, peeled and finely chopped

50g (2oz) cashew nuts

400ml can coconut milk

3 carrots, cut into thin batons

1 broccoli head, cut into florets

20g ($^{3}/_{4}$ oz) fresh coriander, roughly chopped

zest and juice of 1 lime

2 large handfuls of washed spinach leaves

basmati rice to serve

Thai Vegetable Curry

1 Put the curry paste into a large pan. Add the ginger to the pan with the cashew nuts. Stir over a medium heat for 2–3 minutes.

2 Add the coconut milk, cover and bring to the boil. Stir the carrots into the pan and simmer for 5 minutes, then add the broccoli florets and simmer for a further 5 minutes until tender.

3 Stir the coriander and lime zest into the pan with the spinach. Squeeze the lime juice over and serve with basmati rice.

Serves	EASY		NUTRITIONAL INFORMATION	
4	**Preparation Time** 10 minutes	**Cooking Time** 15 minutes	**Per Serving** 200 calories, 10g fat (of which 2g saturates), 19g carbohydrate, 0.7g salt	Vegetarian Gluten free • Dairy free

Cook's tip

Basmati rice should be washed before cooking to remove excess starch and to give really light, fluffy results. Check out the technique for rinsing rice on page 18.

Tuna with Coriander Rice

250g (9oz) basmati rice

8 x 125g (4oz) tuna steaks

5cm (2in) piece fresh root ginger, peeled and grated

1 tbsp olive oil

100ml (3½ fl oz) orange juice

300g (11oz) pak choi, roughly chopped

a small handful of freshly chopped coriander

ground black pepper

lime wedges to garnish

1 Cook the rice according to the packet instructions. Meanwhile, put the tuna steaks in a shallow dish. Add the ginger, oil and orange juice, and season well with pepper. Turn the tuna over to coat.

2 Heat a non-stick frying pan until really hot. Add four tuna steaks and half the marinade. Cook for 1–2 minutes on each side until just cooked. Repeat with the remaining tuna and marinade. Remove the fish from the pan and keep warm.

3 Add the pak choi to the frying pan and cook for 1–2 minutes until wilted. When the rice is cooked, drain and stir the coriander through. Serve the tuna with the pak choi, rice and pan juices, and garnish with lime wedges.

EASY		NUTRITIONAL INFORMATION		Serves
Preparation Time 5 minutes	**Cooking Time** 10 minutes	**Per Serving** 451 calories, 10g fat (of which 2g saturates), 54g carbohydrate, 0.4g salt	Gluten free Dairy free	**4**

Cod with Oriental Vegetables

4 thick cod fillets, 175g (6oz) each

grated zest of 1 lime

1 tbsp chilli oil

1 tbsp sesame oil

1 red chilli, seeded and chopped (see page 50)

2 garlic cloves, chopped

8 spring onions, trimmed and sliced

125g (4oz) shiitake mushrooms, sliced

225g (8oz) carrots, cut into strips

300g (11oz) pak choi, chopped

2 tbsp soy sauce

salt and ground black pepper

lime wedges to serve

1 Put the cod in a shallow, non-metallic dish. Mix the lime zest with the chilli oil and rub over the fillets. Cover and leave in a cool place for 30 minutes.

2 Heat the sesame oil in a large frying pan, add the chilli, garlic, spring onions, mushrooms and carrots and stir-fry for 2–3 minutes until the vegetables begin to soften. Add the pak choi and stir-fry for 1–2 minutes. Add the soy sauce and cook for a further minute. Season.

3 Meanwhile, grill the cod fillets under a medium-hot grill for 2–3 minutes on each side until the flesh has turned opaque and is firm to the touch.

4 Pile the stir-fried vegetables on top of the cod and serve with lime wedges.

Try Something Different

Replace the cod with any firm-fleshed fish: try salmon, coley (saithe), pollack or whiting.

Serves 4	EASY		NUTRITIONAL INFORMATION	
	Preparation Time 10 minutes, plus 30 minutes marinating	**Cooking Time** about 6 minutes	**Per Serving** 284 calories, 9g fat (of which 1g saturates), 12g carbohydrate, 1.9g salt	Gluten free Dairy free

Salmon with Roasted Vegetables

2 large leeks, cut into chunks

2 large courgettes, sliced

2 fennel bulbs, cut into chunks

125ml (4fl oz) hot vegetable stock

zest of ½ lemon

4 salmon fillets, 100g (3½ oz) each

15g (½ oz) pinenuts, toasted

salt and ground black pepper

1 Preheat the oven to 200°C (180°C fan oven) mark 6. Put the leeks into a roasting tin. Add the courgettes and fennel. Pour over the stock, season well with salt and pepper and roast for 30 minutes or until tender.

2 Meanwhile, sprinkle the lemon zest over the salmon and season. Put on a baking sheet lined with greaseproof paper and cook in the oven with the vegetables for the last 20 minutes of the cooking time.

3 Scatter the pinenuts over the roasted vegetables and mix together well. Divide the vegetables among four plates and top each with a piece of salmon.

Serves	EASY		NUTRITIONAL INFORMATION		
4	**Preparation Time** 10 minutes	**Cooking Time** 30 minutes	**Per Serving** 258 calories, 15g fat (of which 2g saturates), 7g carbohydrate, 0.1g salt		Gluten free Dairy free

Try Something Different

- -

Instead of the medium rice noodles try using
rice vermicelli, or leave out the noodles and serve with
basmati rice.

1 tbsp olive oil

1 onion, finely sliced

3 tbsp laksa paste

200ml (7fl oz) coconut milk

900ml (1½ pints) hot vegetable stock

200g (7oz) baby sweetcorn, halved lengthways

600g (1lb 5oz) piece skinless salmon fillet, cut
into 1cm (½ in) slices

225g (8oz) baby leaf spinach

250g (9oz) medium rice noodles

salt and ground black pepper

Salmon Laksa Curry

For the garnish

2 spring onions, sliced diagonally

2 tbsp freshly chopped coriander

2 limes, halved

1 Heat the oil in a large pan, then add the onion and
fry over a medium heat for 10 minutes, stirring, until
golden. Add the laksa paste and cook for 2 minutes.

2 Add the coconut milk, stock and baby corn, and
season. Bring to the boil, reduce the heat and simmer
for 5 minutes.

3 Add the salmon slices and spinach, stirring to
immerse them in the liquid. Cook for 4 minutes or
until the fish is opaque to the centre.

4 Meanwhile, put the noodles in a large bowl, pour
boiling water over and soak for 30 seconds. Drain,
then stir into the curry. Pour into bowls and garnish
with the onions, coriander and lime. Serve at once.

EASY		NUTRITIONAL INFORMATION		Serves
Preparation Time 10 minutes	**Cooking Time** 25 minutes	**Per Serving** 607 calories, 22g fat (of which 3g saturates), 62g carbohydrate, 3.1g salt	Gluten free Dairy free	**4**

Crispy Duck Salad

6 duck legs, about 200g (7oz) each

2 fresh thyme sprigs

1 tsp peppercorns

2 bay leaves

2 tsp salt

125g (4oz) kumquats

125g (4oz) pecan nuts

finely grated zest and juice of 2 oranges

225g (8oz) cranberries

125g (4oz) caster sugar

4 tbsp white wine vinegar

9 tbsp sunflower oil

3 tbsp walnut oil

salt and ground black pepper

frisée leaves to serve

1 Preheat the oven to 180°C (160°C fan oven) mark 4. Put the duck legs into a large flameproof casserole, cover with cold water and bring to the boil. Simmer for 10 minutes, skim the surface and add the thyme, peppercorns, bay leaves and salt. Cook in the oven for 45 minutes–1 hour until tender. Cool quickly in the liquid and chill overnight.

2 Quarter the kumquats. Put the nuts on a baking sheet and toast lightly under a grill. Put the orange zest in a frying pan with 200ml (7fl oz) orange juice, the cranberries and sugar. Bring to the boil and simmer for 5 minutes or until the cranberries are tender. Strain the juice into a pan, reserving the berries. Bring the juice to the boil and bubble until syrupy, then return the cranberries to the pan.

3 In a small bowl, whisk the vinegar and oils and season with salt and pepper. Add the kumquats to the cranberry mixture with the oil and vinegar dressing and the pecan nuts. Set aside.

4 Skim the fat from the jellied duck liquid and set aside. Cut the duck into thick shreds, leaving the skin on. Just before serving, heat 1 tbsp of the reserved duck fat in a large non-stick frying pan and fry half the duck for 5 minutes or until crisp and brown. Keep warm and repeat with the remaining duck. To serve, toss the duck with the cranberry mixture and serve with salad leaves.

A LITTLE EFFORT		NUTRITIONAL INFORMATION		Serves
Preparation Time 10 minutes, plus cooling and overnight chilling	**Cooking Time** 1½ hours	**Per Serving** 655 calories, 65g fat (of which 11g saturates), 22g carbohydrate, 0.2g salt	Gluten free Dairy free	**8**

Try Something Different

Omit the baby new potatoes and serve with mashed potatoes.

Easy Chicken Casserole

1 fresh rosemary sprig

2 bay leaves

1 small chicken

1 red onion, cut into wedges

2 carrots, cut into chunks

2 leeks, cut into chunks

2 celery sticks, cut into chunks

12 baby new potatoes

900ml (1½ pints) hot vegetable stock

200g (7oz) green beans, trimmed

1 Preheat the oven to 180°C (160°C fan oven) mark 4. Put the herbs and chicken in a large ovenproof and flameproof casserole. Add the onion, carrots, leeks, celery, potatoes and stock. Bring to the boil, then cook in the oven for 45 minutes or until the chicken is cooked. To test the chicken is cooked, pierce the thickest part of the leg with a knife; the juices should run clear.

2 Add the beans and cook for 5 minutes. Spoon the vegetables into six bowls. Carve the chicken and divide among the bowls, and ladle the stock over.

Serves	EASY		NUTRITIONAL INFORMATION	
6	**Preparation Time** 15 minutes	**Cooking Time** 50 minutes	**Per Serving** 323 calories, 18g fat (of which 5g saturates), 17g carbohydrate, 0.9g salt	Gluten free Dairy free

Try Something Different

Replace the apricots with ready-to-eat prunes.

2 tbsp olive oil

4 chicken thighs

1 onion, chopped

1 tbsp olive oil

2 tsp cinnamon

2 tbsp honey

150g (5oz) ready-to-eat dried apricots

75g (3oz) blanched almonds

250ml (9fl oz) hot chicken stock

salt and ground black pepper

freshly chopped flat-leafed parsley to garnish

couscous to serve

Chicken Tagine with Apricots

1 Heat 1 tbsp oil in a large flameproof casserole. Add the chicken thighs and fry for 5 minutes or until brown. Remove from the casserole, set aside and keep warm.

2 Add the onion to the pan with the remaining olive oil and fry for 10 minutes until softened. Return the chicken to the pan with the cinnamon, honey, apricots, almonds and stock. Season well, stir once, then cover and bring to the boil. Simmer for 45 minutes or until the chicken is falling off the bone.

3 Garnish with chopped parsley and serve with couscous.

EASY		NUTRITIONAL INFORMATION		Serves
Preparation Time 5 minutes	**Cooking Time** 1 hour	**Per Serving** 500 calories, 29g fat (of which 5g saturates), 26g carbohydrate, 0.6g salt	Dairy free	**4**

Thai Poached Chicken

2 limes, halved

1.4kg (3lb) chicken

a knob of butter

2 lemongrass stalks, crushed

450ml (³/₄ pint) dry white wine

450ml (³/₄ pint) chicken stock

1 small bunch freshly chopped coriander

salt and ground black pepper

rice and vegetables to serve

1 Preheat the oven to 200°C (180°C fan oven) mark 6. Put 2 lime halves into the cavity of the chicken. Rub the chicken with the butter, and season with salt and pepper. Put into a flameproof casserole.

2 Add the lemongrass and remaining lime to the casserole. Pour in the wine and stock. Cover and cook in the oven for 1 hour. Remove the lid and cook for a further 30 minutes. Scatter the coriander over and serve with rice and vegetables.

Serves	EASY		NUTRITIONAL INFORMATION	
4	**Preparation Time** 5 minutes	**Cooking Time** 1½ hours	**Per Serving** 579 calories, 36g fat (of which 10g saturates), 1g carbohydrate, 1g salt	Gluten free Dairy free

Fennel Pork with Cabbage and Apple

2 tbsp olive oil

¹/₂ tbsp fennel seeds, crushed

1 tbsp freshly chopped sage

4 lean pork medallions, 125g (4oz) each

¹/₂ small red cabbage, shredded

450g (1lb) purple sprouting broccoli, tough ends removed

1 apple, cored and sliced into rings

salt and ground black pepper

1 Put 1 tbsp olive oil in a large shallow bowl. Add the fennel seeds and sage, season and mix well. Add the pork and rub the mixture into the meat.

2 Heat the remaining oil in a wok or large frying pan. Stir-fry the cabbage and broccoli for 6–8 minutes until starting to char.

3 Meanwhile, heat a non-stick griddle until hot and fry the pork for 2–3 minutes on each side until cooked through. Remove and put to one side. Add the apple rings to the pan and griddle for 1–2 minutes on each side until starting to char and caramelise. Serve with the pork and vegetables.

EASY		NUTRITIONAL INFORMATION		Serves
Preparation Time 10 minutes	**Cooking Time** 6–10 minutes	**Per Serving** 276 calories, 12g fat (of which 3g saturates), 9g carbohydrate, 0.3g salt	Gluten free Dairy free	**4**

Lamb with Butter Beans and Spinach

2 tbsp olive oil, plus extra to brush
1 onion, finely sliced
1 garlic clove, crushed
2 x 400g cans butter beans, drained
200g (7oz) fresh spinach
4 small lamb chops
½ lemon, cut into wedges to serve

For the dressing
3 tbsp low-fat natural yogurt
2 tbsp tahini
1 tsp harissa paste
juice of ½ lemon
salt and ground black pepper

1 Heat 1 tbsp olive oil in a large pan. Add the onion and fry over a medium heat for 10 minutes or until soft and golden. Add the garlic, cook for 1 minute, then add the butter beans and spinach, and cook for 1–2 minutes to warm through and wilt the spinach.

2 Meanwhile, brush the lamb chops with a little oil and fry in a separate pan for 3–4 minutes on each side.

3 To make the dressing, put the remaining olive oil in a bowl, add the yogurt, tahini, harissa, lemon juice and 2 tbsp cold water. Season well and mix together.

4 To serve, divide the butter bean mixture among four warmed plates. Top with the lamb chops, add a dollop of dressing and serve with the lemon wedges.

Try Something Different

- -

Use cannellini or flageolet beans instead of butter beans.

EASY		NUTRITIONAL INFORMATION		Serves
Preparation Time 5 minutes	**Cooking Time** 12-15 minutes	**Per Serving** 489 calories, 25g fat (of which 8g saturates), 29g carbohydrate, 2.1g salt	Gluten free Dairy free	4

Special supper menu

▶ **Roasted Tomato Bulgur Salad**
  (see page 66)
▼ **Turkish Lamb Stew**
▶ **Strawberry and Black Pepper Granita**
  (see page 111)

Turkish Lamb Stew

2 tbsp olive oil

400g (14oz) lean lamb fillet, cubed

1 red onion, peeled and sliced

1 garlic clove, peeled and crushed

1 potato, quartered

400g can chopped plum tomatoes

1 red pepper, seeded and sliced

200g (7oz) canned chickpeas, drained and rinsed

1 aubergine, cut into chunks

200ml (7fl oz) lamb stock

1 tbsp red wine vinegar

1 tsp each freshly chopped thyme, rosemary and oregano

8 black olives, halved and pitted

salt and ground black pepper

1 Heat 1 tbsp olive oil in a flameproof casserole and brown the lamb over a high heat. Reduce the heat and add the remaining oil, the onion and garlic, then cook until soft.

2 Preheat the oven to 170°C (150°C fan oven) mark 3. Add the potato, tomatoes, red pepper, chickpeas, aubergine, stock, vinegar and herbs to the pan. Season, stir and bring to the boil. Cover the pan, transfer to the oven and cook for 1–1½ hours until the lamb is tender.

3 About 15 minutes before the end of cooking time, add the olives.

Serves 4	EASY		NUTRITIONAL INFORMATION	
	Preparation Time 10 minutes	**Cooking Time** 1½–2 hours	**Per Serving** 389 calories, 20g fat (of which 7g saturates), 28g carbohydrate, 1.2g salt	Gluten free Dairy free

Try Something Different

Use 400g (14oz) pork escalope cut into strips instead of beef. Cook for 5 minutes before removing from the pan at step 2.

2 tbsp soy sauce

2 tbsp Worcestershire sauce

2 tsp tomato purée

juice of $\frac{1}{2}$ lemon

1 tbsp sesame seeds

1 garlic clove, crushed

400g (14oz) rump steak, sliced

1 tbsp vegetable oil

3 small pak choi, chopped

1 bunch spring onions, sliced

freshly cooked egg noodles or tagliatelle to serve

Sesame Beef

1 In a bowl, mix together the soy sauce, Worcestershire sauce, tomato purée, lemon juice, sesame seeds and garlic. Add the steak and toss to coat.

2 Heat the oil in a large wok or non-stick frying pan until hot. Add the steak and sear well. Remove from the wok and set aside.

3 Add any sauce from the bowl to the wok and heat for 1 minute. Add the pak choi, spring onions and steak, and stir-fry for 5 minutes. Add freshly cooked and drained noodles, toss and serve immediately.

EASY		NUTRITIONAL INFORMATION		Serves
Preparation Time 10 minutes	**Cooking Time** 10 minutes	**Per Serving** 207 calories, 10g fat (of which 3g saturates), 4g carbohydrate, 2g salt	Gluten free Dairy free	**4**

5

Puddings

Get Ahead

Make up to a day beforehand. Put into an airtight container and chill.
To use Take out of the refrigerator and allow to reach room temperature (around 30 minutes) before serving.

Summer Fruit Compote

12 fresh, ripe apricots, halved and stoned

125g (4oz) fresh blueberries

50g (2oz) vanilla sugar

juice of 1 orange

200g (7oz) strawberries, hulled and halved

Greek yogurt to serve

1 Preheat the oven to 180°C (160°C fan oven) mark 4. Put the apricots, blueberries, sugar and orange juice into a large, shallow baking dish and bake, uncovered, for about 20 minutes or until just tender.

2 Gently stir in the strawberries. Taste the cooking juices – you may want to add a little extra sugar – then leave to cool. Cover and chill. Serve with a spoonful of Greek yogurt.

Serves 4	EASY		NUTRITIONAL INFORMATION	
	Preparation Time 10 minutes	**Cooking Time** 20 minutes, plus cooling and chilling	**Per Serving** 122 calories, trace fat (of which 0g saturates), 30g carbohydrate, 0g salt	Vegetarian Gluten free

Strawberry and Black Pepper Granita

400g (14oz) hulled strawberries

75g (3oz) golden caster sugar

juice of $\frac{1}{2}$ lemon

ground black pepper

1 Whiz the strawberries to a purée in a food processor or blender. Add the sugar, lemon juice and a good grinding of black pepper. Stir in 450ml ($\frac{3}{4}$ pint) water. Pulse to mix, then pour into a freezerproof container.

2 Freeze for 2 hours. Use a fork to stir in the frozen edges then freeze again for 1 hour. Fork through, then freeze for a further 1 hour or overnight. Use a fork to break up the granita, then serve in tall glasses.

EASY	NUTRITIONAL INFORMATION		Serves
Preparation Time 10 minutes, plus freezing	**Per Serving** 67 calories, trace fat (of which 0g saturates), 17g carbohydrate, 0g salt	Vegetarian Gluten free • Dairy free	**6**

Try Something Different

Use a cinnamon stick instead of the star anise.

Nectarines in Spiced Honey and Lemon

4 tbsp clear honey

2 star anise

1 tbsp freshly squeezed lemon juice

150ml (¼ pint) boiling water

4 ripe nectarines or peaches, halved and stoned

vanilla ice cream to serve

1 Put the honey, star anise and lemon juice in a heatproof bowl. Stir in the boiling water and leave until just warm.

2 Add the nectarines or peaches to the bowl and leave to cool. Transfer to a glass serving dish. Serve with a scoop of vanilla ice cream.

Serves 4	EASY		NUTRITIONAL INFORMATION	
	Preparation Time 10 minutes, plus cooling		**Per Serving** 95 calories, trace fat (of which 0g saturates), 23g carbohydrate, 0g salt	Vegetarian Gluten free • Dairy free

Try Something Different

This is just as good with mangoes and orange syrup; use 1 orange instead of 2 limes.

Papaya with Lime Syrup

75g (3oz) golden caster sugar
zest and juice of 2 limes
2 papayas, peeled, halved and seeds removed

1 Put the sugar in a small pan with 100ml (3½ fl oz) water and the lime zest and juice. Heat gently to dissolve the sugar, then bring to the boil and bubble rapidly for 5 minutes or until the mixture is reduced and syrupy.

2 Cut the papayas into slices and arrange on a large serving plate. Drizzle over the lime syrup and serve.

EASY		NUTRITIONAL INFORMATION		Serves
Preparation Time 10 minutes	**Cooking Time** 10 minutes	**Per Serving** 200 calories, trace fat (of which 0g saturates), 50g carbohydrate, 0g salt	Vegetarian Gluten free • Dairy free	**4**

Special supper menu

▶ **Tomato, Pepper and Orange Soup (see page 45)**

▶ **Tuna with Coriander Rice (see page 93)**

▼ **Summer Pudding**

Summer Pudding

800g (1lb 12oz) mixed summer berries, such as 250g (9oz) each redcurrants and blackcurrants and 300g (11oz) raspberries

125g (4oz) golden caster sugar

3 tbsp crème de cassis

9 thick slices of slightly stale white bread, crusts removed

1 Put the redcurrants and blackcurrants into a medium pan. Add the sugar and cassis. Bring to a simmer and cook for 3–5 minutes until the sugar has dissolved. Add the raspberries and cook for 2 minutes. Once the fruit is cooked, taste it – there should be a good balance between tart and sweet.

2 Meanwhile, line a 1 litre (1³/₄ pint) bowl with clingfilm. Put the base of the bowl on one piece of bread and cut around it. Put the circle of bread in the base of the bowl.

3 Line the inside of the bowl with more slices of bread, slightly overlapping to avoid any gaps. Spoon in the fruit, making sure the juice soaks into the bread. Keep back a few spoonfuls of juice in case the bread is unevenly soaked when you turn out the pudding.

4 Cut the remaining bread to fit the top of the pudding neatly, using a sharp knife to trim any excess bread from around the edges. Wrap in clingfilm, weigh down with a saucer and a tin can, and chill overnight.

5 To serve, unwrap the outer clingfilm, upturn the pudding on to a plate and remove the inner clingfilm. Drizzle over the reserved juice and serve with crème fraîche or clotted cream.

EASY		NUTRITIONAL INFORMATION		Serves
Preparation Time 10 minutes, plus overnight chilling	**Cooking Time** 10 minutes	**Per Serving** 173 calories, 1g fat (of which trace saturates), 38g carbohydrate, 0.4g salt	Vegetarian Dairy free	**8**

Try Something Different

If watermelon is not in season use another variety of melon, such as Charentais, Canteloupe or Galia. If you are using one of the sweeter varieties, reduce the honey to about 1 tbsp.

Watermelon with Feta and Honey

2 tbsp pinenuts

½ watermelon

50g (2oz) feta cheese

2 tbsp clear honey

a handful of roughly chopped mint

1 Put the pinenuts in a small pan and toast over a medium-high heat, tossing occasionally, until golden-brown all over, about 2–3 minutes. Cool.

2 Cut the rind off the watermelon, and cut into chunks. Arrange on a serving plate. Crumble the feta cheese over the melon and drizzle the honey over.

3 Scatter with the pinenuts and mint.

Serves 4	EASY		NUTRITIONAL INFORMATION	
	Preparation Time 10 minutes	**Cooking Time** 3 minutes	**Per Serving** 182 calories, 8g fat (of which 2g saturates), 24g carbohydrate, 0.5g salt	Vegetarian Gluten free

Cook's tip

Use thick-skinned oranges for this recipe, as they're the easiest to peel.

Oranges with Caramel Sauce

6 oranges

25g (1oz) butter

2 tbsp golden caster sugar

2 tbsp Grand Marnier

2 tbsp orange marmalade

zest and juice of 1 large orange

crème fraîche to serve

1 Preheat the oven to 200°C (180°C fan oven) mark 6. Cut away the peel and pith from the oranges, then put them into a roasting tin just large enough to hold them.

2 Melt the butter in a pan and add the sugar, Grand Marnier, marmalade, orange zest and juice, then heat gently to dissolve the sugar. Pour over the oranges. Bake for 30–40 minutes. Serve with crème fraîche.

EASY		NUTRITIONAL INFORMATION		Serves
Preparation Time 15 minutes	**Cooking Time** 40 minutes	**Per Serving** 139 calories, 4g fat (of which 2g saturates), 24g carbohydrate, 0.1g salt	Vegetarian Gluten free • Dairy free	**6**

Tropical Fruit Pots

400g can apricots in fruit juice

2 balls of stem ginger in syrup, finely chopped, plus 2 tbsp syrup from the jar

½ tsp ground cinnamon

juice of 1 orange

3 oranges, cut into segments

1 mango, peeled, stoned and chopped

1 pineapple, peeled, core removed and chopped

450g (1lb) coconut yogurt

3 tbsp lemon curd

3–4 tbsp light muscovado sugar

1 Drain the juice from the apricots into a pan and stir in the syrup from the ginger. Add the chopped stem ginger, ground cinnamon and orange juice. Put over a low heat and stir gently. Bring to the boil and simmer for 2–3 minutes to make a thick syrup.

2 Roughly chop the apricots and put into a bowl with the segmented oranges, mango and pineapple. Pour over the syrup. Divide among eight 300ml (½ pint) glasses or dessert bowls.

3 Beat the yogurt and lemon curd together in a bowl until smooth. Spoon a generous dollop over the fruit and sprinkle with muscovado sugar, or chill if not serving immediately.

Get Ahead

The fruit salad can be made and left to marinate up to 4 hours before you plan to eat – no need to chill.

Serves 8	EASY		NUTRITIONAL INFORMATION	
	Preparation Time 15 minutes	**Cooking Time** 5 minutes	**Per Serving** 192 calories, 1g fat (of which trace saturates), 45g carbohydrate, 0.1g salt	Vegetarian Gluten free

Freezing Tip

Put the fruit and syrup into a freezerproof container, leave to cool, then cover with a tight-fitting lid and freeze for up to three months.
To use Thaw overnight in the refrigerator and serve cold.

Spiced Winter Fruit

150ml (¼ pint) port

150ml (¼ pint) freshly squeezed orange juice

75g (3oz) soft light brown sugar

1 cinnamon stick

6 whole cardamom pods, lightly crushed

5cm (2in) piece fresh root ginger, peeled and thinly sliced

50g (2oz) large muscatel raisins or dried blueberries

1 small pineapple, peeled, core removed and thinly sliced

1 mango, peeled, stoned and thickly sliced

3 tangerines, peeled and halved horizontally

3 fresh figs, halved

1 First, make the syrup. Pour the port and orange juice into a small pan, then add the sugar and 300ml (½ pint) cold water. Bring to the boil, stirring all the time. Add the cinnamon stick, cardamom pods and ginger, then bubble gently for 15 minutes.

2 Put all the fruit in a serving bowl. Remove the cinnamon stick and cardamom pods from the syrup – or leave in for a spicier flavour – then pour over the fruit. Serve cold.

Serves 6	EASY		NUTRITIONAL INFORMATION	
	Preparation Time 20 minutes	**Cooking Time** 20 minutes, plus cooling	**Per Serving** 207 calories, trace fat (of which 0g saturates), 45g carbohydrate, 0g salt	Vegetarian Gluten free • Dairy free

Try Something Different

Use nectarines instead of peaches, and raspberries or blueberries instead of strawberries.

Poached Peaches and Strawberries

4 ripe peaches, halved, stoned and quartered

250ml (9fl oz) orange juice

½ tbsp golden caster sugar

a small pinch of ground cinnamon

225g (8oz) halved strawberries

1 Put the peaches in a pan with the orange juice, sugar and cinnamon. Simmer gently for 5 minutes. Remove the peaches with a slotted spoon and put in a bowl.

2 Let the juice bubble until reduced by half. Pour over the peaches, then cool, cover and chill. Remove from the refrigerator about 2 hours before serving and stir in the halved strawberries.

EASY		NUTRITIONAL INFORMATION		Serves
Preparation Time	**Cooking Time**	**Per Serving**	Vegetarian	**4**
10 minutes, plus chilling	10 minutes, plus cooling and chilling	82 calories, trace fat (of which 0g saturates), 19g carbohydrate, 0g salt	Gluten free • Dairy free	

Baked Apricots with Almonds

12 apricots, halved and stoned
3 tbsp golden caster sugar
2 tbsp amaretto liqueur
25g (1oz) unsalted butter
25g (1oz) flaked almonds
crème fraîche to serve

1 Preheat the oven to 200°C (180°C fan oven) mark 6. Put the apricot halves, cut-side up, in an ovenproof dish. Sprinkle with the sugar, drizzle with the liqueur, then dot each apricot half with a little butter. Scatter the flaked almonds over them.

2 Bake in the oven for 20–25 minutes until the apricots are soft and the juices are syrupy. Serve warm, with crème fraîche.

Try Something Different

Use nectarines or peaches instead of apricots.

EASY		NUTRITIONAL INFORMATION		Serves
Preparation Time 5 minutes	**Cooking Time** 20-25 minutes	**Per Serving** 124 calories, 6g fat (of which 2g saturates), 16g carbohydrate, 0.1g salt	Vegetarian Gluten free • Dairy free	**6**

Chocolate Cherry Roll

4 tbsp cocoa

100ml (3½ fl oz) milk, plus 3 tbsp

5 medium eggs, separated

125g (4oz) golden caster sugar

400g can pitted cherries

1–2 tbsp cherry jam

cocoa and icing sugar to dust

1 Preheat the oven to 180°C (160°C fan oven) mark 4 and line a 30.5 x 20.5cm (12 x 8in) Swiss-roll tin with baking parchment. Mix the cocoa and 3 tbsp milk in a bowl. Heat 100ml (3½ fl oz) milk in a pan until almost boiling. Add to the bowl, stirring. Cool for 10 minutes.

2 Whisk the egg whites in a clean grease-free bowl until soft peaks form. Whisk together the egg yolks and sugar until pale and thick, then gradually whisk in the cooled milk. Fold in the egg whites. Spoon into the prepared tin and level the surface. Bake for 25 minutes or until just firm.

3 Turn out on to a board lined with baking parchment and leave to cool for 5 minutes, then loosely roll up and leave until cold. Unroll. Drain the cherries and chop them. Spread the cherry jam over the roulade and top with the cherries. Roll up from the shortest end. Dust with cocoa and icing sugar, cut into slices and serve.

Try Something Different

Raspberries make a great alternative to cherries: use 350g (12oz) fresh raspberries and 1 tbsp raspberry jam.

Serves	FOR THE CONFIDENT COOK		NUTRITIONAL INFORMATION	
8	**Preparation Time** 15 minutes	**Cooking Time** 25–30 minutes, plus cooling	**Per Serving** 180 calories, 5g fat (of which 2g saturates), 29g carbohydrate, 0.3g salt	Vegetarian Gluten free

Apple and Blueberry Strudel

700g (1½ lb) red apples, quartered, cored and thickly sliced

1 tbsp lemon juice

2 tbsp golden caster sugar

100g (3½ oz) dried blueberries

1 tbsp olive oil

6 sheets of filo pastry, thawed if frozen

crème fraîche to serve

1 Preheat the oven to 190°C (170°C fan oven) mark 5. Put the apples into a bowl and mix with the lemon juice, 1 tbsp sugar and the blueberries.

2 Warm the olive oil. Lay three sheets of filo pastry side by side, overlapping the long edges. Brush with the oil. Cover with three more sheets of filo and brush again.

3 Tip the apple mixture on to the pastry and roll up from a long edge. Put on to a non-stick baking sheet. Brush with the remaining oil and sprinkle with the remaining caster sugar. Bake for 40 minutes or until the pastry is golden and the apples soft. Serve with crème fraîche.

Serves	EASY		NUTRITIONAL INFORMATION	
6	**Preparation Time** 15 minutes	**Cooking Time** 40 minutes	**Per Serving** 178 calories, 2g fat (of which trace saturates), 40g carbohydrate, 0g salt	Vegetarian Dairy free

Glossary

Al dente Italian term commonly used to describe food, especially pasta and vegetables, which are cooked until tender but still firm to the bite.

Baking blind Pre-baking a pastry case before filling. The pastry case is lined with greaseproof paper and weighted down with dried beans or ceramic baking beans.

Baste To spoon the juices and melted fat over meat, poultry, game or vegetables during roasting to keep them moist. The term is also used to describe spooning over a marinade.

Beat To incorporate air into an ingredient or mixture by agitating it vigorously with a spoon, fork, whisk or electric mixer. The technique is also used to soften ingredients.

Bind To mix beaten egg or other liquid into a dry mixture to hold it together.

Blanch To immerse food briefly in fast-boiling water to loosen skins, such as peaches or tomatoes, or to remove bitterness, or to destroy enzymes and preserve the colour, flavour and texture of vegetables (especially prior to freezing).

Bouquet garni Small bunch of herbs – usually a mixture of parsley stems, thyme and a bay leaf – tied in muslin and used to flavour stocks, soups and stews.

Braise To cook meat, poultry, game or vegetables slowly in a small amount of liquid in a pan or casserole with a tight-fitting lid. The food is usually first browned in oil or fat.

Caramelise To heat sugar or sugar syrup slowly until it is brown in colour; ie forms a caramel.

Chill To cool food in the fridge.

Compote Fresh or dried fruit stewed in sugar syrup. Served hot or cold.

Coulis A smooth fruit or vegetable purée, thinned if necessary to a pouring consistency.

Cream To beat together fat and sugar until the mixture is pale and fluffy, and resembles whipped cream in texture and colour. The method is used in cakes and puddings which contain a high proportion of fat and require the incorporation of a lot of air.

Croûtons Small pieces of fried or toasted bread, served with soups and salads.

Crudités Raw vegetables, usually cut into slices or sticks, typically served with a dipping sauce.

Curdle To cause sauces or creamed mixtures to separate, usually by overheating or over-beating.

Cure To preserve fish, meat or poultry by smoking, drying or salting.

Deglaze To heat stock, wine or other liquid with the cooking juices left in the pan after roasting or sautéeing, scraping and stirring vigorously to dissolve the sediment on the bottom of the pan.

Dice To cut food into small cubes.

Dredge To sprinkle food generously with flour, sugar, icing sugar etc.

Dust To sprinkle lightly with flour, cornflour, icing sugar etc.

Escalope Thin slice of meat, such as pork, veal or turkey, from the top of the leg, usually pan-fried.

Fillet Term used to describe boned breasts of birds, boned sides of fish, and the undercut of a loin of beef, lamb, pork or veal.

Flake To separate food, such as cooked fish, into natural pieces.

Folding in Method of combining a whisked or creamed mixture with other ingredients by cutting and folding so that it retains its lightness. A large metal spoon or plastic-bladed spatula is used.

Fry To cook food in hot fat or oil. There are various methods: shallow-frying in a little fat in a shallow pan; deep-frying where the food is totally immersed in oil; dry-frying in which fatty foods are cooked in a non-stick pan without extra fat; see also Stir-frying.

Garnish A decoration, usually edible, such as parsley or lemon, which is used to enhance the appearance of a savoury dish.

Gluten A protein constituent of grains, such as wheat and rye, which develops when the flour is missed with water to give the dough elasticity.

Griddle A flat, heavy, metal plate used on the hob for cooking scones or for searing savoury ingredients.

Gut To clean out the entrails from fish.

Hull To remove the stalk and calyx from soft fruits, such as strawberries.

Infuse To immerse flavourings, such as aromatic vegetables, herbs, spices and vanilla, in a liquid to impart flavour. Usually the infused liquid is brought to the boil, then left to stand for a while.

Julienne Fine 'matchstick' strips of vegetables or citrus zest, sometimes used as a garnish.

Macerate To soften and flavour raw or dried foods by soaking in a liquid, eg soaking fruit in alcohol.

Marinate To soak raw meat, poultry or game – usually in a mixture of oil, wine, vinegar and flavourings – to soften and impart flavour. The mixture, which is known as a marinade, may also be used to baste the food during cooking.

Medallion Small round piece of meat, usually beef or veal.

Mince To cut food into very fine pieces, using a mincer, food processor or knife.

Parboil To boil a vegetable or other food for part of its cooking time before finishing it by another method.

Pare To finely peel the skin or zest from vegetables or fruit.

Poach To cook food gently in liquid at simmering point; the surface should be just trembling.

Pot roast To cook meat in a covered pan with some fat and a little liquid.

Purée To pound, sieve or liquidise vegetables, fish or fruit to a smooth pulp. Purées often form the basis for soups and sauces.

Reduce To fast-boil stock or other liquid in an uncovered pan to evaporate water and concentrate the flavour.

Refresh To cool hot vegetables very quickly by plunging into ice-cold water or holding under cold running water in order to stop the cooking process and preserve the colour.

Roast To cook food by dry heat in the oven.

Roux A mixture of equal quantities of butter (or other fat) and flour cooked together to form the basis of many sauces.

Rubbing in Method of incorporating fat into flour by rubbing between the fingertips, used when a short texture is required. Used for pastry, cakes, scones and biscuits.

Salsa Piquant sauce made from chopped fresh vegetables and sometimes fruit.

Sauté To cook food in a small quantity of fat over a high heat, shaking the pan constantly – usually in a sauté pan (a frying pan with straight sides and a wide base).

Scald To pour boiling water over food to clean it, or loosen skin, eg tomatoes. Also used to describe heating milk to just below boiling point.

Score To cut parallel lines in the surface of food, such as fish (or the fat layer on meat), to improve its appearance or help it cook more quickly.

Sear To brown meat quickly in a little hot fat before grilling or roasting.

Seasoned flour Flour mixed with a little salt and pepper, used for dusting meat, fish etc., before frying.

Shred To grate cheese or slice vegetables into very fine pieces or strips.

Sieve To press food through a perforated sieve to obtain a smooth texture.

Sift To shake dry ingredients through a sieve to remove lumps.

Simmer To keep a liquid just below boiling point.

Skim To remove froth, scum or fat from the surface of stock, gravy, stews, jam etc. Use either a skimmer, a spoon or kitchen paper.

Steam To cook food in steam, usually in a steamer over rapidly boiling water.

Steep To immerse food in warm or cold liquid to soften it, and sometimes to draw out strong flavours.

Stew To cook food, such as tougher cuts of meat, in flavoured liquid which is kept at simmering point.

Stir-fry To cook small even-sized pieces of food rapidly in a little fat, tossing constantly over a high heat.

Sweat To cook chopped or sliced vegetables in a little fat without liquid in a covered pan over a low heat to soften.

Tepid The term used to describe temperature at approximately blood heat, ie 37°C (98.7°F).

Vanilla sugar Sugar in which a vanilla pod has been stored to impart its flavour.

Whipping (whisking) Beating air rapidly into a mixture either with a manual or electric whisk. Whipping usually refers to cream.

Zest The thin coloured outer layer of citrus fruit, which can be removed in fine strips with a zester.

Index